(Continued)

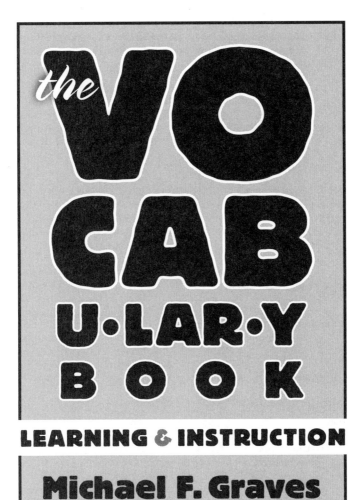

the VOCAB-U·LAR·Y BOOK

LEARNING & INSTRUCTION

Michael F. Graves

TEACHERS COLLEGE PRESS
Teachers College
Columbia University
New York and London

INTERNATIONAL
Reading Association
800 BARKSDALE ROAD, PO BOX 8139
NEWARK, DE 19714-8139, USA

NCTE
National Council of
Teachers of English
Urbana, IL

Published simultanesouly by Teachers College Press, 1234 Amsterdam Avenue, New York, NY 10027; The International Reading Association, 800 Barksdale Road, Newark, DE 19714; and the National Council of Teachers of English, 1111 W. Kenyon Road, Urbana, IL 61801-1596

Grateful acknowledgment is made for the following:

In Chapter 3: Material from Juel, C. et al (2004, March) Making Words Stick. *Educational Leadership 61*(6), p. 30. The Association for Supervision and Curriculum Development is a worldwide community of educators advocating sound policies and sharing best practices to achieve the success of each learner. To learn more, visit ASCD at www.ascd.org.
In Chapter 4: Passage (p. 22) from Nagy, William E. (1988). *Teaching Vocabulary to Improve Reading Comprehension*. Newark, DE: International Reading Association. Reprinted with permission of the International Reading Association.
In Chapter 4: Material from R. J. Ryder and Michael Graves, *Reading and Learning in Content Areas*. Copyright © 2003 by John Wiley & Sons, Inc. This material is used by permission of John Wiley & Sons, Inc.
In Chapter 5: Material from Michael Graves, Connie Juel, and Bonnie Graves, *Teaching Reading in the 21st Century (with Assessment and Instruction Booklet)*, 3rd ed. Published by Allyn and Bacon, Boston, MA. Copyright © 2004 by Pearson Education. Reprinted by permission of the publisher.

Library of Congress Cataloging-in-Publication Data

Graves, Michael F.
    The vocabulary book : learning and instruction / Michael F. Graves.
       p. cm. — (Language and literacy series)
    Includes bibliographical references and index.
    ISBN 0-8077-4628-2 (cloth)—ISBN 0-8077-4627-4 (paper)
    1. Vocabulary—Study and teaching. I. Title. II. Language and literacy series (New York, N.Y.)

    LB1574.5.G72 2006
    372.6'61—dc22   2005050095

ISBN 13:   ISBN 10:
978-0-8077-4627-1 (paper)   0-8077-4627-4 (paper)
978-0-8077-4628-8 (cloth)   0-8077-4628-2 (cloth)

NCTE stock number 56282
IRA inventory number 9214

Printed on acid-free paper. Manufactured in the United States of America.

13 12 11 10 09 08 07 06   8 7 6 5 4

To Bonnie

Contents

CHAPTER 1

Introduction

The importance of vocabulary is daily demonstrated in schools and out. In the classroom, the achieving students possess the most adequate vocabularies. Because of the verbal nature of most classroom activities, knowledge of words and ability to use language are essential to success in these activities. After schooling has ended, adequacy of vocabulary is almost equally essential for achievement in vocations and in society.

Walter Petty, Curtis Herold, and Earline Stoll, English Educators

Shortly before or after they celebrate their first birthday, children are likely to utter their first word. Establishing just when children say their first word isn't easy for a number of reasons. For one thing, children aren't always considerate enough to say their first word when an adult is conveniently present to record it. For another, children's first words usually appear after a period of extensive babbling of nonsense sounds, and true words aren't always easy to distinguish from babbling. And for still another, children's first words are usually recorded by their parents, and proud parents can be somewhat less than objective observers of their offspring's accomplishments.

Although we often cannot pinpoint when exactly a child utters her first word, child language specialists such as Clark (1993) can tell us a lot about children's early vocabularies. Syntactically, early words may represent sentences; to a child the word *ball* may actually mean "Bring me the ball," "That's a ball," or "Throw the ball." Semantically, early words may represent broader meanings than do similar adult words. *Juice* may be used to refer to milk, water, and anything else that children drink. Alternately, early words may represent narrower meanings than do similar adult words. *Dog* may be applied to large dogs such as German Shepherds and Irish Setters, but not to small dogs such as Chihuahua and Pekingese. And in some cases, children both underextend and overextend word meanings, as when *dog* is used only for large dogs but is also used to refer to sheep, cows, goats, and horses. Nor is the first set of meanings that children assign to a word all that predictable. One boy first used the term *wah wah* to refer to dogs and then used it to refer to all animals, soft slippers, and a picture of an old man dressed in fur.

After uttering their first word, children initially accumulate new words rather slowly. Over the 3 months following the appearance of the first word, they may learn an additional 50 words. During this period, many children speak exclusively in one-word utterances. Then, after accumulating the 50 or so words, they begin stringing words together to form sentences, two-word sentences at first, then three-word sentences, and soon longer ones. By Age 2, many children have productive vocabularies of 500–600 words and receptive vocabularies considerably larger than that.

Vocabulary and other facets of language develop rapidly after this point. By the time children enter first grade, their phonological systems are largely or fully complete. Although not all first graders have achieved phonemic awareness and although their phonics skills are just beginning to develop, most first graders can recognize and produce all or almost all of the sounds in their language. Their syntactic systems, although not as advanced as their phonological systems, are well on their way to maturity. Few 6-year-olds have mastered the most complex syntactic structures, but most can understand and produce a large percentage of the nearly infinite number of sentence patterns in the language. At this time, children's vocabulary development is in one sense similarly impressive: They have learned a very large number of words. However, their vocabulary learning has really only begun. Between the time they enter first grade and the time they graduate from high school, students will add tens of thousands of words to their vocabularies.

Before considering more of what is known about children's vocabularies, it is useful to consider the importance of vocabulary, the topic that Petty, Herold, and Stoll (1967) discussed in the introductory quote to this chapter. Virtually all authorities on literacy education agree strongly with Petty and his colleagues that vocabulary knowledge is vital to success in reading, in literacy more generally, in school, and in the world outside of school. The findings of over 100 years of vocabulary research include the following:

- Vocabulary knowledge is one of the best indicators of verbal ability (Sternberg, 1987; Terman, 1916).
- Vocabulary knowledge contributes to young children's phonological awareness, which in turn contributes to their word recognition (Goswami, 2001; Nagy, 2005).

- Vocabulary knowledge in kindergarten and first grade is a significant predictor of reading comprehension in the middle and secondary grades (Cunningham & Stanovich, 1997; Scarborough, 1998).
- Vocabulary difficulty strongly influences the readability of text (Chall & Dale, 1995; Klare, 1984).
- Teaching vocabulary can improve reading comprehension for both native English speakers (Beck, Perfetti, & McKeown, 1982) and English learners (Carlo et al., 2004).
- Growing up in poverty can seriously restrict the vocabulary children learn before beginning school, and can make attaining an adequate vocabulary a challenging task (Coyne, Simmons, & Kame'enui, 2004; Hart & Risley, 1995).
- Disadvantaged students* are likely to have substantially smaller vocabularies than their more advantaged classmates (Templin, 1957; White, Graves, & Slater, 1990).
- Learning English vocabulary is one of the most crucial tasks for English learners (Folse, 2004; Nation, 2001).
- Lack of vocabulary can be a crucial factor underlying the school failure of disadvantaged students (Becker, 1977; Biemiller, 1999).

Fortunately, since vocabulary is so important, we know a great deal about vocabulary development and about how to teach vocabulary. The 100 years of vocabulary research have led to a wealth of findings in addition to the list above. I review the research on vocabulary learning and vocabulary instruction in some detail in Chapter 2, and I use both the vocabulary research and the many recommendations that have been made about teaching vocabulary throughout this book. At this point, however, I want to introduce three crucial facts about vocabulary, facts to keep in mind when reading this book and planning vocabulary instruction.

1. *The vocabulary learning task is enormous!* Estimates of vocabulary size vary greatly, but a reasonable estimate based on a substantial

---

*By *disadvantaged students* I refer to students who grew up in environments in which they are likely to have encountered fewer English words than their more advantaged peers. Many of these students grew up in poverty and many grew up in homes in which English was not the primary language. The term does not imply that these students, the language they speak at home, or their communities are somehow less good or less worthy than other students, the language they speak at home, or their communities. However—and this is the main point that we need to keep in mind and do something about—in school many disadvantaged students will encounter more unfamiliar words than their more advantaged classmates.

body of recent and rigorous work (Anderson & Nagy, 1992; Anglin, 1993; Miller & Wakefield, 1993; Nagy & Anderson, 1984; Nagy & Herman, 1987; White et al., 1990) is this: The books and other reading materials used by school children include over 180,000 different words. The average child enters school with a very small reading vocabulary, typically consisting largely of environmental print. Once in school, however, a child's reading vocabulary is likely to soar at a rate of 3,000–4,000 words a year, leading to a reading vocabulary of something like 25,000 words by the time she is in eighth grade, and a reading vocabulary of something like 50,000 words by the end of high school.

2. *That there are far more words to be learned than we can possibly teach is not an argument that we should not teach any of them* (Beck, McKeown, & Omanson, 1987). Both instruction on individual words and instruction that promotes children's ability and propensity to learn words on their own are very worthwhile (Baumann & Kame'enui, 2004; Carlo, August, & Snow, 2005; Folse, 2004; Graves, 2000; Kamil & Hiebert, 2005; Nagy, 2005; National Reading Panel, 2000; Osborn & Lehr, in press; RAND Reading Study Group, 2002; Stahl, 1998).

3. *There is increasing evidence that many children of poverty enter school with vocabularies much smaller than those of their middle-class counterparts.* There is also evidence that having a small vocabulary is a very serious detriment to success in reading (Chall, Jacobs, & Baldwin, 1990; Cunningham & Stanovich, 1997; Hirsch, 2003; Scarborough, 1998). These two facts make it especially important to find ways to bolster the oral and reading vocabularies of students who enter school with small stores of words (Baumann, Kame'enui, & Ash, 2003; Becker, 1977; Biemiller, 1999, 2001, 2004; Coyne, Simmons, & Kame'enui, 2004; Hart & Risley, 1995, 2003; National Reading Panel, 2000; RAND Reading Study Group, 2002; White et al., 1990). For similar reasons, bolstering the English vocabularies of English learners is critically important (Carlo et al., 2005; Folse, 2004; Nation, 2001; Schmitt, 2000).

A FOUR-PART VOCABULARY PROGRAM

This book presents a comprehensive plan for vocabulary instruction that is broad enough to include all children: children who enter school with relatively small vocabularies; English learners with small English vocabularies; children who possess adequate but not exceptional vocabularies; and children who already have rich and powerful vocabularies and are prepared for the challenge of developing still more sophisticated and useful vocabularies. More specifically, the book describes a four-part vocabulary program that I began developing 20 years ago (Graves, 1984, 1985) and have continued to modify and hone since that time (Graves, 1987, 1992, 2000, 2004; Graves & Fitzgerald, in press; Graves & Slater, in press; Graves & Watts, 2002). In its present form, the program has the following four components: (1) providing rich and varied language experiences; (2) teaching individual words; (3) teaching word-learning strategies; and (4) fostering word consciousness. In the next several sections, I briefly discuss each component and the rationale behind it.

Providing Rich and Varied Language Experiences

One way to build students' vocabularies is to immerse them in a rich array of language experiences so that they learn words through listening, speaking, reading, and writing. In kindergarten and the primary grades, listening and speaking are particularly important for promoting vocabulary growth. Most children enter kindergarten with substantial oral vocabularies and very small reading vocabularies. Appropriately, most of the words in materials they read are words that are already in their oral vocabularies (Biemiller, 2004; McKeown & Beck, 2004). For this reason, however, young children will not learn many new words from reading; they will learn them from discussion, from being read to, and from having attention directly focused on words. In the intermediate grades, middle school, and secondary school, discussion continues to be important. Students of all ages—English learners as well as native English speakers—need to engage frequently in authentic discussions, give-and-take conversations in which they get the opportunity to thoughtfully discuss topics (Alvermann, 2000). Increasingly from the intermediate grades on, reading becomes the principle language experience for enlarging students' vocabularies (Cunningham & Stanovich, 1998). If we can substantially increase the reading students do, we can substantially increase the words they learn. Thus one way to help students enlarge their vocabularies is to increase the amount of reading they do (Anderson, 1996). In fact, some researchers (e.g., Anderson & Nagy, 1992; Stahl, 1998) believe that increasing the amount that students read is the single most powerful thing teachers can do to increase their vocabularies, and this may well be the case. Anyone interested in increasing students' vocabularies should do everything possible to see that they read as much and as widely as possible.

Teaching Individual Words

Another way to help students increase their vocabularies is to teach them individual words. To be sure, the enormous size of the vocabulary that students will eventually attain means that we cannot teach all of the words they need to learn. However, as already noted, the fact that teachers cannot teach all of the words students need to learn does not mean that they cannot and should not teach some of them (Beck, McKeown, & Omanson, 1987; Folse, 2004; Graves, 2000; Nagy, 2005; Nation, 2001; Stahl, 1998). Research has revealed a good deal about effective—and ineffective—approaches to teaching individual words (e.g., see, Baumann, Kame'enui, & Ash, 2003; Beck & McKeown, 1991; Herman & Dole, 1988; Nagy, 1988, 2005; Stahl & Fairbanks, 1986): Vocabulary instruction is most effective when learners are given both definitional and contextual information, when learners actively process the new word meanings, and when they experience multiple encounters with the words. In other words, vocabulary instruction is most effective, and is most likely to influence students' comprehension, when it is rich, deep, and extended (McKeown & Beck, 2004).

Unfortunately, effective vocabulary instruction is not as frequent or as robust as it should be in classrooms (Durkin, 1978/79; Scott, Jamieson-Noel, & Asselin, 2003; Watts, 1995) or in basal readers (Durkin, 1981; Ryder & Graves, 1994; Walsh, 2003). But help is available: A good deal of recent writing on vocabulary instruction incorporates these research findings, often along with some other considerations. Biemiller (2001, 2004) proposes a program of direct instruction on specific words. Nagy (1988) suggests methods specifically selected to improve reading comprehension. Blachowicz and Fisher (1996) emphasize ways of including vocabulary instruction in all classrooms. And I (Graves, 2000; Graves, Juel, & Graves, 2004; Graves & Slater, in press) suggest different methods for different learning goals, including: teaching students to read words already in their oral vocabularies; teaching new labels for known concepts; teaching words representing new concepts; and clarifying and enriching the meanings of already known words.

Teaching Word-Learning Strategies

A third approach to help students increase their vocabularies is to teach word-learning strategies. The most widely recommended strategy is that of using context (Graves, 2000; Stahl, 1998; Sternberg, 1987). Recent reviews of research (Baumann, Kame'enui, et al., 2003; Fukkink & de Glopper, 1998; Kuhn & Stahl, 1998) indicate that this strategy can be taught. And several studies (Baumann, Edwards, Boland, Olejnik, & Kame'enui, 2003; Baumann et al., 2002; Blachowicz & Zabroske, 1990; Buikema & Graves, 1993) describe research-based ways of doing so.

Using word parts to unlock the meanings of unknown words is another widely recommended strategy (Blachowicz & Fisher, 1996; Edwards, Font, Baumann, & Boland, 2004), and doing so is well supported by research (Anglin, 1993; Baumann, Font, Edwards, & Boland, 2005; White, Power, & White, 1989). I describe some research-based procedures for teaching prefixes (Graves, 2004). White, Sowell, and Yanagihara (1989) discuss research-based procedures for teaching prefixes and suffixes. And Edwards and her colleagues (2004) discuss research-based procedures for teaching prefixes, suffixes, and roots.

Using the dictionary is a third recommended approach (Blachowicz & Fisher, 1996; Graves et al., 2004) that students can use to learn word meanings by themselves, and the same authors who recommend teaching students to use the dictionary have suggested what needs to be taught and learned.

Fostering Word Consciousness

The last component of the four-part program is fostering word consciousness. The term *word consciousness* refers to an awareness of and interest in words and their meanings. As defined by Anderson and Nagy (1992), word consciousness involves both a cognitive and an affective stance toward words. Word consciousness integrates metacognition about words, motivation to learn words, and deep and lasting interest in words.

Students who are word conscious are aware of the words around them—those they read and hear and those they write and speak. This awareness involves an appreciation of the power of words, an understanding of why certain words are used instead of others, and a sense of the words that could be used in place of those selected by a writer or speaker. It also involves, as Scott and Nagy (2004) emphasize, recognition of the communicative power of words, of the differences between spoken and written language, and of the particular importance of word choice in written language. And it involves an interest in learning and using new words and becoming more skillful and precise in word usage.

With something like 50,000 words to learn and with most of this word learning taking place incidentally as students are reading and listening, a positive disposition toward words is crucial. Word consciousness exists at many levels of complexity and sophistication, and can and should be fostered among preschoolers as well as among students in and beyond high school.

AN OVERVIEW OF THIS BOOK

The remainder of this book consists of six chapters, each of which is briefly described below.

Chapter 2, "Words and Word Learning," begins with a discussion of the vocabulary learning task students face and then moves to a discussion of vocabulary instruction. The latter discussion includes considerations of the vocabulary instruction in schools, instruction for linguistically disadvantaged students, teaching individual words, teaching word-learning strategies, fostering word consciousness, and vocabulary instruction for English learners.

Chapter 3, "Providing Rich and Varied Language Experiences," deals with the first part of the four-part program. The first section of the chapter stresses the importance of promoting incidental word learning and discusses ways of doing so through listening, discussion, reading, and writing. The second section of the chapter discusses how to directly build primary-grade children's oral vocabularies through interactive oral reading. In doing so, it first discusses characteristics of effective approaches to interactive oral reading and then discusses four specific approaches to interactive oral reading for use in the classroom. The chapter concludes with a brief discussion of word consciousness activities for primary-grade children.

Chapter 4, "Teaching Individual Words," describes the second part of the program. The first section of the chapter discusses several preliminaries to teaching individual words, including the number of words students must learn, levels of word knowledge, the various word-learning tasks that different words represent, identifying and selecting vocabulary to teach, and some principles of vocabulary instruction. The second and much longer section of the chapter presents detailed descriptions of specific procedures for accomplishing the various word-learning tasks. The third section discusses ways of selecting among the different teaching procedures and notes which ones are particularly effective in improving reading comprehension.

Chapter 5, "Teaching Word-Learning Strategies," describes the third part of the program. This chapter describes powerful procedures for teaching students to use context, word parts, and the dictionary to infer and learn word meanings. It also describes an approach students can use in dealing with unknown words they meet in reading, suggests some personal approaches students can take to build their vocabularies, and considers when and by whom word-learning strategies should be taught.

Chapter 6, "Promoting Word Consciousness," deals with the fourth and final part of the program. The approaches described include modeling and encouraging adept diction, promoting word play, providing rich and expressive instruction, involving students in original investigations, and teaching students about words. The chapter includes both spontaneous approaches, which require relatively little time from students or the teacher, and thoroughly planned and robust approaches, which require significant amounts of time from students and teachers.

Chapter 7, "Classroom Portraits of Effective Vocabulary Instruction," presents classroom portraits of vocabulary learning and instruction in the primary grades, the intermediate grades, middle school, and high school.

CHAPTER 2

Words and Word Learning

Everything should be as simple as it can be, but no simpler.

Albert Einstein

Einstein's aphorism perfectly defines my goal as I write this chapter—to keep the theory and research on vocabulary as simple as possible without downplaying its importance to vocabulary instruction. The study of vocabulary has all too frequently been an atheoretical endeavor (Clifford, 1978), and vocabulary instruction has often lacked underlying principles to guide it (Hiebert, 2005). As a consequence, a lot of the suggestions for vocabulary instruction found in books and journals and a lot of the vocabulary instruction taking place in schools is ineffective. The theory and research briefly described here will empower educators to develop vocabulary instruction that is principled, efficient, and effective. In this chapter, I take up two major topics, first considering the vocabulary learning task that students face across the K–12 years and then considering the research on vocabulary instruction.

THE VOCABULARY LEARNING
TASK STUDENTS FACE

One of the first steps in planning a vocabulary program is to understand the learning task students face. To do this requires consideration of just what is meant by the term *word*, what it means to know a word, how many words are likely to occur in the materials students read, and how many words students are likely to know at various grade levels. In this section, I consider each of these matters in turn.

What Is a Word?

Philosophers, linguists, and educators have grappled with the question of what constitutes a word over a considerable period of time and in considerable depth, and it is certainly not my goal to answer that question in a definitive way here. Instead, I want to explain how the term will be used in this book, particularly in discussions of how many words students know or need to learn. Even to do this, we need to distinguish among several types of vocabulary. Vocabulary can be classified as receptive (words we understand when others use them) or productive (words we use themselves). Vocabulary can also be classified as oral or written. Thus each of us has four vocabularies: receptive-oral, words we understand when we hear them; receptive-written, words we can read; productive-oral, words we use in our speech; and productive-written, words we use in our writing. The four vocabularies overlap but are not the same, and the relationships between them change over time. Children entering school, for example, have very large oral vocabularies but very small reading vocabularies. Literate adults, on the other hand, have larger reading vocabularies than oral vocabularies. And both children and adults have larger receptive vocabularies than productive ones; that is, they understand more words when they hear or read them than they use in their speech or writing. The emphasis in this book will be on reading vocabulary; however, all four types of vocabulary are important, and I will give some attention to each of them.

In order to talk about vocabulary size—the very important matter of how many words students know and need to learn—it is also necessary to decide just what we will call a word. When written, words are groups of letters separated by white space. Thus *the* is a word, *apple* another word, *predawn* another, *perpendicular* another, and *houseboat* still another. Unfortunately, by this same definition *want, wants, wanted,* and *wanting* are also different words. However, for the most part, when I am considering how many words student know or need to learn, I will use the term *word* to refer to *word families,* by which I mean the basic word and its inflected forms. Thus when I say that children add something like 3,000 words to their reading vocabularies each year they are in school, I will be counting the forms *want, wants, wanted,* and *wanting* as a single word.

Another convention I will follow in talking about the size of the learning task is to count graphic forms with different meanings as a single word. Thus *key* referring to a door key, *key* the musical term, and *key* meaning a small island are considered one word. Doing so definitely underestimates the size of the learning task, but it is necessary because the convention is followed in virtually all studies of vocabulary size.

What Does It Mean to Know a Word?

In order to discuss topics like how many words students know and how to teach words, it is also necessary to consider what it means to know a word. A number of vocabulary scholars have considered this question, and they are all in agreement on one matter: Words can be known at various levels. For example, Beck, McKeown, and Kucan (2002) list five levels:

- No knowledge
- General sense, such as knowing *mendacious* has a negative connotation
- Narrow, context-bound knowledge, such as knowing that a *radiant* bride is a beautifully smiling happy one, but unable to describe an individual in a different context as radiant
- Having knowledge of a word but not being able to recall it readily enough to apply it in appropriate situations
- Rich, decontextualized knowledge of a word's meaning, its relationship to other words, and its extension to metaphorical uses, such as understanding what someone is doing when they are *devouring* a book (p. 10)

This scale makes good sense, and I refer to it again in Chapter 4 when I discuss how different instructional procedures produce different levels of learning. But there is more to be said about what it means to know a word. Some years ago Cronbach (1942) noted that knowing a word involves the ability to select situations in which it is appropriately applied, recall different meanings of the word, and recognize exactly in what situations the word does not apply. More recently, Calfee and Drum (1986) noted that knowing a word well "involves depth of meaning; precision of meaning; facile access (think of scrabble and crossword puzzle experts); the ability to articulate one's understanding; flexibility in the application of the knowledge of a word; the appreciation of metaphor, analogy, word play; the ability to recognize a synonym, to define, to use a word expressively" (pp. 825–826).

Nagy and Scott (2000) further underscore the complexity of what it means to know a word when they discuss five aspects of the complexity of word knowledge: incrementality, polysemy, multidimensionality, interrelatedness, and heterogeneity. I will discuss each of these in some detail in Chapter 6 when I discuss the sorts of knowledge about words that students need to develop. But I believe that the main message of this section is clear: Words can be known at various levels, and fully learning a word is a multifaceted task.

How Many Words Are There?

In the most serious attempt to get a reliable estimate of how many words there are in contemporary American English, Nagy and Anderson completed a study appropriately titled "How Many Words Are There in Printed School English" (1984). They used as their source *The American Heritage Word Frequency Book* (Carroll, Davies, & Richman, 1971), a very well done compilation of the words occurring in books and other material likely to be used by children in Grades 3–9. Based on careful study and a number of calculations, Nagy and Anderson concluded that printed school English contains about 88,000 word families. Subsequent to the original study, Anderson and Nagy (1992) again considered the size of printed school English and concluded that if proper nouns, multiple meanings of words, and idioms were included, their estimate would increase to 180,000 word families.

More recently, Zeno, Ivens, Millard, and Duvvuri (1995) produced *The Educator's Word Frequency Guide*, basically an updated version of the earlier *Word Frequency Book* based on a much larger corpus of material used in kindergarten through college. No one has yet calculated the number of word families in the *Educator's Word Frequency Guide*, but since the number of entries in the *Guide* is considerably larger than the number in the *Word Frequency Book*, it is reasonable to assume that an estimate based on the *Guide* would be well over 180,000.

Note that these are not estimates of the size of individual students' vocabularies; they are estimates of the number of words in the myriad texts students might encounter. Note also that many of these words are extremely rare and no single student will encounter all of them, much less learn all of them. Still, realizing that there are this many words that could be taught is important; it is very clear that we cannot directly teach all of them.

How Many Words Do Students Learn?

Estimates of the number of words in students' reading vocabularies vary more than as estimates of the total number of words that exist. They range from lows of 2,000 words for third graders and 7,800 words for twelfth graders (Dupuy, 1974) to highs of 26,000 words for first graders (Shibles, 1959) and over 200,000 words for college freshmen (Hartman, 1946). These extreme estimates can be dismissed, or at least very strongly questioned, because of such factors as the size of the dictionary from which words were sampled, the definition of what constitutes a word, the method of testing, the sampling procedures used, and such ad hoc requirements as that a word appear in a number of different dictionaries (Graves, 1986; Lorge & Chall, 1963).

In my judgment, the most unbiased estimate of the size of students' reading vocabularies comes from work done by Nagy and Herman (1987). Using data gathered from the Nagy and Anderson 1984 study, Nagy and Herman recalibrated earlier estimates and concluded that third graders' reading vocabularies average about 10,000 words, that twelfth graders' reading vocabularies average about 40,000 words, and that school children therefore learn about 3,000 words each year. These figures refer to word families as previously described, but they do not include idioms, multiple meanings, or proper nouns, which would raise the figure considerably. All in all, my best estimate—based on the work of Anderson and Nagy, 1992; Anglin, 1993; Miller and Wakefield, 1993; Nagy and Anderson, 1984; Nagy and Herman, 1987; and White, Graves, and Slater, 1990—is that average twelfth graders know something like 50,000 word families and learn from 3,000 to 4,000 words each year. These figures, however, are for average or above average students. A number of studies (e.g., Biemiller & Slonim, 2001; Hart & Risley, 1995; Templin, 1957; White et al., 1990) have demonstrated large differences between the vocabularies of linguistically advantaged and linguistically disadvantaged students. A reasonable estimate is that linguistically advantaged students enter first grade with an oral vocabulary of perhaps 10,000 words and leave high school with a reading and oral vocabulary in the 50,000 word range, while linguistically disadvantaged students both enter and leave school with vocabularies of about half that size. The goal is to help all students develop an extensive vocabulary—something like 50,000 words—over the school years. This of course means that some students begin school with a much larger learning task, a topic that I address directly in Chapter 3.

One other fact about the vocabulary learning task students face is crucial. The English language includes a very large number of infrequent words and a very small number of frequent words. Here are some examples of just how important frequent words are: The first 100 words in Fry's (2004) Instant Words list—an empirically derived list of frequent words—account for 50% of the words in school materials. The first 300 words in that list account for 65% of the words in school materials. The first 5,000 words in *The American Heritage Word Frequency Book* (Carroll et al., 1971) account for nearly 90% of the words in materials for Grades 3 to 9. And the first 5,000 words in *The Educator's Word Frequency Guide* (Zeno et al., 1995) account for nearly 80% of the words in materials for kindergarten through college (Kamil & Hiebert, 2005). The fact that a relatively small number of frequent words account for so many of the words students will encounter in texts means that students must know these words well, if they are to avoid repeatedly stumbling over them and in so doing fail to understand what they read.

As I see it, the bottom line with respect to the number of words students eventually learn and what to do about helping them learn them is this: There are far too many words to teach all of them directly, but there is a much smaller number of frequent words, which can be taught directly. Teaching 1,000 to 3,000 of the most frequent words directly, or at least ensuring that all children know these words as soon as possible, is a feasible task. Beyond those 1,000 to 3,000 words, there are simply too many words available to choose words to teach based on their frequency and systematically teach them. Instead, once students have learned the 1,000 to 3,000 most frequent words—which means before the end of third grade for most students (but not for English learners with small English vocabularies or native English speakers with small vocabularies)—we need to select words to teach from the material students are reading or listening to. That is, select vocabulary to teach from important words students don't know in the material they are reading or listening to. Such instruction can teach students some important words, assist them in understanding and learning from the material they are reading or listening to, and repeatedly remind them of the importance of vocabulary. I discuss how to teach the most frequent 1,000 to 3,000 words and how to choose words from learning materials and teach them in Chapters 3 and 4.

VOCABULARY INSTRUCTION

In this section I consider research on the vocabulary instruction that typically takes place in schools, instruction for linguistically disadvantaged children, teaching individual words, teaching word-learning strategies, fostering word consciousness, and teaching vocabulary to English learners.

The Vocabulary Instruction in Schools

There are a handful of studies on vocabulary instruction in basal readers and a similar number on the vocabulary instruction that actually takes place in the classroom.

In an analysis of basal readers done some 25 years ago, Beck, McKeown, McCaslin, and Burkes (1979) examined the vocabulary instruction presented in the third through sixth grades in two basal reader series and found that much of the instruction was weak. In summarizing their work, Beck, McCaslin, and McKeown (1980) described the best and the worst instruction that could be expected to occur in the series:

> [At best] a new vocabulary word is presented in a sentence that elucidates the meaning of the new word; the word is encountered in the text selection and the student looks it up in the glossary if s/he does not remember its meaning; the word appears a third time in an independently completed, after reading activity. . . .
>
> At worst, a new word appears solely in a selection and the student skips over it because s/he either does not recognize it as an unknown word or does not want to be bothered with the disruption of the glossary. (pp. 7–8)

Several years later, Durkin (1981) investigated the attention given to vocabulary in the kindergarten through Grade 6 teacher's manuals of five basal reader series. She concluded that there was "limited attention given to new vocabulary, especially in the middle- and upper-grade manuals" (p. 525) and suggested that "manuals and teachers may need to do much more with new words before children attempt to read a selection" (526).

In a slightly later analysis of basal readers, Jenkins and Dixon (1983) examined the instruction in several fourth-grade texts and reached a similar negative conclusion. They also noted that even with the strongest texts they examined, students would only learn about 300 words a year from the basal reader programs, a small fraction of the total number of words students need to learn.

In the most recent formal study of vocabulary instruction in basal readers, Randall Ryder and I (Ryder & Graves, 1994) analyzed the vocabulary instruction presented prior to reading in the fourth- and sixth-grade books of two series. We found that the instruction in these basals was superior to what other investigators had found in earlier series but did not appear to be sufficiently powerful to improve comprehension of the upcoming selections.

Finally, in an essay based on her review of the five most widely used basal reading programs, Walsh (2003) notes that "none even attempts the kind of sustained building of word and domain knowledge that is essential for increased reading comprehension" (p. 24). Although this is a strong personal judgment and not a result supported by a formal research study, it is certainly true that little robust and sustained building of word knowledge is found in basals.

Although the body of literature on vocabulary instruction in basals is small and the latest study a decade old, it appears that the instruction provided in basals is improving but there is still a great deal of room for improvement.

The literature on the vocabulary instruction in classrooms also consists of a handful of studies. In an extensive study of fourth-grade classrooms aimed primarily at investigating comprehension instruction, Durkin (1978/79) found that out of 4,469 minutes of observation only 19 minutes were devoted to vocabulary instruction with an additional 4 minutes devoted to vocabulary review. Obviously, in the classrooms Durkin observed, vocabulary instruction played a very small role.

In a slightly later study Roser and Juel (1982) found that out of 1,200 minutes of observation of first- through fifth-grade classrooms, only 65 minutes—or 5% of the time—was given to vocabulary instruction. Roser and Juel further noted that word meaning instruction per lesson ranged from 0 to 12 minutes, with many lessons containing no vocabulary instruction at all.

A decade later Watts (1995) observed three third-grade classrooms and three sixth-grade classrooms in an urban school to explore how teachers taught meaning vocabulary during reading lessons and what purposes teachers had when teaching vocabulary. Watts found that most vocabulary was taught as a prereading activity; that in 87% of the cases teachers presented definitional information about the words and in 37% of the cases they presented contextual information on the words (Watts categories were not mutually exclusive); and that "characteristics associated with effective instruction in the research literature such as activation of prior knowledge, multiple exposures, and provision of strategies for independent word learning were rarely observed" (p. 399). She also found that teachers generally saw the purpose of vocabulary instruction as assisting students with the selection being read and not in terms of the more general goal of building students' vocabularies in ways that would be beneficial both in and out of school.

In the most recent study of vocabulary instruction in schools I am familiar with, Scott, Jamieson-Noel, and Asselin (2003) observed vocabulary instruction in 23 fourth- through eighth-grade classrooms in Canada.

Their results showed that about 12% of the time devoted to literacy activities was given to vocabulary instruction, but that only 1.4 percent of the time spent on academic subjects other than language arts (math, science, art, and social studies) was spent on vocabulary instruction. Their results also showed that although instruction in keeping with the research literature was more common than in previous studies, most instruction still involved mentioning meanings and assigning vocabulary to be learned, rather than providing solid instruction in vocabulary.

Considering both the vocabulary instruction in basal readers and that observed in actual classrooms, the situation appears to be this: The vocabulary instruction in basals and the vocabulary instruction in classrooms more generally has improved over the past 25 years. However, there remains a great deal of room for improvement. The sorts of powerful vocabulary instruction documented in the research need to become more common, vocabulary instruction needs to become more frequent in academic areas such as science and social studies, and something needs to be done to help students with relatively small vocabularies catch up with their classmates. Moreover, although I know of no formal research on vocabulary instruction in secondary schools, I spend a good deal of time in secondary schools and with secondary teachers and can testify that there is little vocabulary instruction at that level and that what there is generally consists of providing students with definitions.

Instruction for Linguistically Disadvantaged Children

As I have noted, studies have consistently shown large differences between the vocabularies of linguistically advantaged and linguistically disadvantaged children (Biemiller & Slonim, 2001; Hart & Risley, 1995; Templin, 1957; White et al., 1990). A number of educators (e.g., Becker, 1977; Biemiller, 2001; Chall, Jacobs, & Baldwin, 1990; Hart & Risley, 2003) have viewed less advantaged students' smaller vocabularies as a major barrier to school success. As a consequence, there have been a number of attempts to bolster the vocabularies of less advantaged students during the preschool or primary-grade years. The most successful of these attempts have been ones that employ *interactive oral reading*—reading in which adults read to children, periodically stopping to highlight and discuss individual words and sometimes other aspects of what they are reading.

In an early study Whitehurst and his colleagues (1988) trained parents "to increase their rates of open-ended questions, function/attribute questions, and expansions; to respond appropriately to children's attempts to answer these questions; and to decrease their frequency of straight reading and questions that could be answered by pointing" (p. 552). Results of a one-month, home-based intervention in which the effects produced by these trained parents were compared to those obtained by parents in an uninstructed control group showed that children of the trained parents scored significantly higher on standardized tests of expressive language ability. In a more recent study Biemiller (2003) trained teachers of kindergarten to second-grade students to read with their students using the following procedures: Stories were read once without interruption; they were then read three more times on 3 subsequent days with target words explained; after each reading, teachers reread the sentences containing the target words and again explained them. Results on a posttest showed substantial word learning and better word learning than was found when the stories were not first read without interruption, when there were fewer readings and therefore fewer target word explanations, and when teachers rather than children explained the words.

In Chapter 3 I discuss in some detail several interactive oral reading programs—Dialogic Reading (Whitehurst et al., 1988), Direct and Systematic Instruction (Biemiller, 2001, 2003), Text Talk (Beck & McKeown, 2001), and Anchored Instruction (Juel & Deffes, 2004). Here, I want to note that this is an extremely important type of vocabulary instruction for children who enter school with relatively small vocabularies, and that a number of studies, including those just cited, have shown that interactive oral reading successfully teaches word meanings. However, these results must be taken as encouraging rather than definitive. All of the studies have been relatively short, and none of them have taught anything like the number of words that less advantaged students need to learn in order to catch up to their more advantaged peers. Instruction that successfully bridges this gap will need to extend over several years and teach many more words than have been taught thus far.

Teaching Individual Words

There is a large, robust, easily interpretable, and very consistent body of research on teaching individual words. There are also a number of important summaries of the research on vocabulary instruction. These include traditional reviews of research by Petty, Herold, and Stoll (1967), Mezynski (1983), myself (Graves, 1986), Beck and McKeown (1991), Blachowicz and Fisher (2000), the National Reading Panel (2000), and Baumann, Kame'enui, and Ash (2003); and a meta-analysis by Stahl and Fairbanks (1986). As Nagy (2005) has recently noted, we know a great deal about teaching vocabulary. Moreover, as I just noted, the findings are very consistent. In the remainder of this section I make a series of research-based generalizations and support each generalization with a representative study or several studies. In organizing the generalizations, I proceed from considering effects that can be achieved by brief and relatively shallow instruction to effects that can be achieved from more lengthy and more powerful instruction.

Some vocabulary instruction is better than no instruction (Baumann, Kame'enui, & Ash, 2003; Petty et al., 1967). Although this is a commonsense finding, it is not a trivial one. It means that vocabulary instruction typically works. However, "thin instruction"—for example, giving students a set of words and asking them to look up the words in the dictionary, or giving them a set of words and their definitions—only serves to teach the basic meanings of the words. That is, simply giving students definitions of words will not result in their learning rich and full meanings, is unlikely to improve their comprehension of the text from which the words were selected, and is unlikely to result in their actively using the words in their speech or writing. In one study involving thin instruction, Parker (1984) pretaught sixth-, seventh-, and eighth-grade students 10 words out of two short social studies selections over a 2-day period and tested them the day after they received the instruction and 3 weeks later. As part of the study, he compared a dictionary definition treatment in which students simply looked up the words in a dictionary and wrote out their definitions with no instruction. Results indicated that students receiving the dictionary treatment scored about twice as well as the control group immediately after the instruction and about 50% better than the control group 3 weeks later. Although Parker tested students 3 weeks after the instruction, most of the research that employs thin instruction is short term and tests students' knowledge of the words taught within a few days or a week of the instruction. Whether or not students forget many of the words learned from thin instruction over time is a definite question.

Instruction that incorporates both definitional information and contextual information is likely to be stronger than instruction incorporating only one sort of information (Mezynski, 1983; Stahl & Fairbanks, 1986). While simply having students work with definitions of words can improve their word knowledge, giving them both definitional information and contextual information has repeatedly proved a stronger approach. In fact, except in situations where there are far too

many unknown words in an upcoming selection to teach and it is necessary to give students a glossary, using a procedure that gives students
both definitional and contextual information is the thinnest approach
I recommend. In one study, Stahl (1983) worked with fifth graders and
compared the results of a definition-only treatment, a definition-plus-
context treatment, and no instruction. In the definition-only treatment,
students looked up words in the dictionary, wrote definitions of the
words, and discussed their meanings. In the definition-plus-context
treatment, students also worked with context. And in the no-instruc-
tion treatment, students simply took the pre- and posttests. Results
indicated that the definition-only treatment was superior to no instruction but that the definition-plus-context treatment was superior to no
instruction and to the definition-only treatment.

*Instruction that involves activating prior knowledge and compar-
ing and contrasting word meanings is likely to be more powerful than
simple combinations of contextual information and definitions* (Beck
& McKeown, 1991; Baumann, Kame'enui, & Ash, 2003). Not only is instruction that involves activating prior knowledge and comparing and
contrasting word meanings a powerful approach to teaching word meanings, but such instruction has also been shown to improve comprehension of selections containing the words taught. The best known and most
widely researched techniques falling in this category are Semantic
Mapping (Heimlich & Pittelman, 1986) and Semantic Feature Analysis (Pittelman, Heimlich, Berglund, & French, 1991). In a study of Semantic Mapping with third-, fourth-, and fifth-grade students, Johnson,
Toms-Bronowski, and Pittelman (1982) found that students receiving
semantic mapping instruction significantly outperformed students in
a context group on both immediate and delayed measures. In investigating the effects of Semantic Feature Analysis, Anders, Bos, and Filip
(1984) found that learning disabled high school students learned more
vocabulary and better comprehended a social studies passage containing the taught vocabulary than did students who looked up words in
the dictionary and wrote out their definitions.

*More lengthy and robust instruction that involves active learning,
inferences, prior knowledge, and frequent encounters, is likely to be
more powerful than less time-consuming and less robust instruction* (Beck et al., 2002; Nagy, 2005). While Semantic Mapping and
Semantic Feature Analysis are quite robust sorts of vocabulary instruction, Beck and McKeown and their colleagues have developed, refined,
and repeatedly tested several forms of Rich Vocabulary Instruction that

involves students in extensive and varied experiences with words (Beck et al., 1982; McKeown, Beck, Omanson, & Perfetti, 1983; McKeown, Beck, Omanson, & Pople, 1985; Beck & McKeown, 2004). In the initial study in the sequence (Beck et al., 1982), fourth-grade students from an urban school were taught 104 words over a period of 5 months. The words were grouped into semantic sets (for example, the People set included the words *accomplice, virtuoso, rival, miser, philanthropist, novice, hermit,* and *tyrant*), with each set taught over a 5-day cycle that included many varied activities. On Day 1 of a cycle, students were introduced to the words, wrote the words and their definitions in their logbooks, and used the words in one or two ways. On Day 2, students generated sentences for each word and did a fairly easy activity that involved word meaning. On Day 3, they generally generated contexts in which the new words could be used. On Day 4, they did speeded trials with the words in a gamelike situation. On Day 5, they took a multiple-choice test on the words. Outside of class, attention to the words was motivated by a gamelike activity in which students received points for bringing in evidence that they had seen, heard, or used the target words outside of class. In all, students received 10–18 encounters with some words and 26–40 encounters with others. Results indicated that compared to uninstructed students, instructed students learned the words better, were faster and more accurate in timed responses to the words, and demonstrated marginal gains in comprehension. Results also showed that more encounters with the words produced more learning.

Later studies by Beck and McKeown and their colleagues confirmed the positive results of the initial study and also produced additional information on Rich Instruction. Another study with fourth graders (McKeown et al., 1983), which involved approximately 30 minutes of Rich Instruction per word, showed that instructed students demonstrated substantially better comprehension of passages containing the taught words compared to uninstructed students. And still another study with fourth graders (McKeown et al., 1985), this one involving up to 15 minutes of Rich Instruction per word, showed that 12 encounters produced stronger results than 4 encounters and that students who also used the words outside of the classroom learned them more fully that those who did not.

In the most recent iteration of their work, Beck and McKeown (2004) used Rich Instruction in teaching oral vocabulary to kindergarten and first-grade children as part of Text Talk, an interactive oral reading procedure I describe in Chapter 3. The work included two studies. In the first study, children receiving the Text Talk instruction achieved significantly higher scores on the vocabulary posttest than did students in the comparison group, learning about 70% of the words taught. In the second study, children again used Text Talk but received more instruction with the words. In all, they received 5 encounters with some words and 20 encounters with others. Results indicated that more encounters produced more learning. However, even with 20 encounters, students did not learn 100% of the words taught.

Taken together, the studies by Beck and McKeown and their colleagues clearly show that teaching vocabulary can improve comprehension, that Rich Instruction in which students have multiple thoughtful encounters with words is very worthwhile, and that more encounters with words produces better learning than fewer encounters. However, it needs to be remembered that Rich Instruction comes at a huge cost. It may require up to 30 minutes per word and involve activities outside of class as well as in class. Clearly, we cannot provide Rich Instruction for all of the words we need to teach.

Teaching Word-Learning Strategies

The three word-learning strategies of concern here are (1) teaching students to use context to infer the meanings of unknown words; (2) teaching students to use word parts to glean word meanings; and (3) teaching students to use the dictionary. There is a fair amount of research on using context and word parts. There is very little research on teaching students to use the dictionary, but there is some research on dictionaries themselves that is relevant to instructional considerations. There are also a number of reviews of research on context and somewhat fewer on word parts. These include traditional reviews and meta-analyses by myself (Graves, 1986), Beck and McKeown (1991), Fukkink and de Glopper (1998), Kuhn and Stahl (1998), Swanborn and de Glopper (1999), Baumann, Kame'enui, and Ash (2003), and Baumann, Font, Edwards, and Boland (2005). In what follows, I take up the use of context, word parts, and the dictionary in turn.

Context Clues. Relevant studies on context clues include descriptive research on students' ability to use context to learn the meanings of unknown words and instructional research that attempts to improve students' ability to use context to learn word meanings. As Sternberg (1987) has pointed out, "Most vocabulary is learned from context" (p. 89). In my judgment and that of most other vocabulary researchers, no other explanation can account for the huge number of words students learn. In what follows, I first consider studies that tended to employ more artificial learning situations, and then studies that used more natural situations.

At the artificial end of the continuum and in what appears to be the earliest study of children's ability to use context, Werner and Kaplan (1952) asked 9–13-year-old children to determine the meaning of a pseudo word from a series of six sentences, each of which provided further information about the word's meaning. Although the task proved to be a difficult one and children at different ages showed differential ability to determine meaning, children of all ages learned some meaning from context. In a less artificial study but one that still directly prompted students to use context as they were reading, Shefelbine (1983) alerted sixth-grade students to the possibility of using context clues, gave them a brief example of how to do so, and then read short passages from a basal reader to them, promoting them to use the context to figure out the meaning of a difficult word in the passage. Results indicated that students did learn from context under these conditions.

In a somewhat more natural study, Carroll and Drum (1983) first asked eleventh and twelfth graders to define 40 words and then had them read natural passages containing one occurrence of 20 of the words and again define all of them. Posttest results indicated that students achieved some learning from context. In another somewhat more natural study, Jenkins, Stein, and Wysocki (1984) presented fifth graders with artificial passages containing 0, 2, 6, and 10 occurrences of target words without alerting students to the fact that the study dealt with vocabulary. Results indicated that 6 to 10 occurrences of the words were required to produce gains on the vocabulary measures used. In a follow-up study, Jenkins and Wysocki (1985) presented sixth graders with similar passages and found that 5 occurrences were necessary to produce vocabulary gains.

The studies described thus far show that students can derive word meanings from context when deliberately prompted to do so. A more important skill and a more natural task is that of inferring word meaning from context when not deliberately prompted to do so. Two studies by Nagy and his colleagues were the first to address this important task. In the first study, Nagy, Herman, and Anderson (1985) asked eighth-grade students to read two natural passages containing one or two occurrences of difficult words without alerting students to the fact that the study dealt with vocabulary. Results indicated that the probability of students learning a word's meaning well enough to answer a multiple-choice item was .15. In a follow-up study, which improved on the methodology of the earlier one, Nagy, Anderson, and Herman (1987) had students read four natural passages and found that the probability of students learning a word well enough to answer a multiple-choice question was .05. They also found that "there was simply no learning from context for words at the highest level of conceptual difficulty" (p. 225).

Nagy and his colleagues consider the probability of .05 yielded by the second study the more likely one. However, they argue that even though the probability of learning a word from context is small, given the volume of reading students do, they learn a very large number of words from context. Based on their 1985 findings, they estimated that the typical middle-grade student annually learns between 1,500 and 8,000 words from context. Based on their 1987 findings, they estimated that the average middle-grade child learns between 800 and 1,200 words from context annually. Although these two estimates are very different, both show substantial learning from context.

Based on a meta-analysis of 20 studies of students' learning from context when not directly prompted to do so, Swanborn and de Glopper (1999) concluded that students can and do learn words incidentally from context and that the probability of learning a word from one exposure in naturally occurring context is .15. They also showed that students at higher grade levels and students with higher reading ability are better able to use context, and that texts containing fewer unknown words better facilitate learning from context.

All in all, the descriptive research on learning from context shows that context can produce learning of word meanings and that although the probability of learning a word from a single occurrence is low, the probability of learning a word from context increases substantially with additional occurrences of the word. That is how we typically learn from context. We learn a little from the first encounter with a word and then more and more about a word's meaning as we meet it in new and different contexts.

The next question to consider is whether students can be taught to better use context to learn the meanings of unknown words. As Baumann, Kame'enui, and Ash (2003) point out, not all instruction in using context clues has been successful. In fact, teaching students to use context clues is a challenging task. Still, there have been some notable successes. In one early study, Carnine, Kame'enui, and Coyle (1984) used both a rule-plus-practice and a practice-only treatment, both of which were very brief, and found that either treatment facilitated students' ability to use context in a passage constructed by the experimenters. In another early study Patberg, Graves, and Stibbe (1984) used an active teaching approach to teach fifth-grade students to use synonym clues and contrast clues. The instruction required three 30-minute sessions. Results indicated that the instructed students outperformed students in a practice-only group and students in an uninstructed control group in determining the meanings of untaught new words presented in short texts containing the sorts of clues taught. However, in a follow-up study Patberg and Stibbe (1985) found no effects of instruction in using context clues.

In a more recent study, Janice Buikema and I (Buikema & Graves, 1993) taught seventh- and eighth-grade students to use a particular strategy for unlocking the meanings of unknown words in context over the period of a week. Although our instruction focused on one type of context clue— descriptive clues—our emphasis was on using the strategy rather than on the clue type. The instructed students outperformed uninstructed control group students in their ability to infer word meanings from context on several measures, including one that used natural context.

Two recent studies by Baumann and his associates (Baumann, Edwards, et al., 2003; Baumann et al., 2002) are the most ambitious to date. Both studies taught contextual analysis and morphological analysis. In the 2002 study fifth graders were assigned to a morphemic-only group, a context-only group, a combined morphemic-context group, or an uninstructed control group. Students received twelve 50-minute lessons, which followed an explicit instruction model (verbal explanation, modeling, guided practice, and independent practice), included gradual release of responsibility, and provided students with declarative, procedural, and conditional knowledge about the strategy they were learning. Results indicated that students in both the contextual group and the morphemic group were better able to glean the meanings of transfer words on an immediate test, but not on a delayed test.

In the 2003 study fifth-grade students were given a combined contextual and morphological analysis treatment and received it embedded in the context of their social studies lessons. Their learning was then compared to that of students who were taught the vocabulary of the social studies texts in a traditional fashion. Results indicated that students receiving the experimental treatment were more successful at inferring the meanings of novel affixed words and at inferring the meanings of morphologically and contextually decipherable words on a delayed test but not on an immediate test.

Based on a 1998 meta-analysis of 21 studies of instruction in context clues, Fukkink and de Glopper concluded that instruction aimed at enhancing the skill of deriving word meaning from context during reading does have a positive effect. Although Fukkink and de Glopper could not include the 2002 and 2003 studies of Baumann and his associates, the results of doing so would have been the same.

Taken together, the studies on students' ability to use context to learn word meanings produce the following findings: Students of all ages do learn word meanings from context; the chance of doing so in a single encounter is low but increases with increased encounters; and instruction aimed at students ability to use context to infer meanings of novel words can be successful. As I mentioned earlier, however, and as this review demonstrates, teaching students to use context clues is a substantial task. Consistent with suggestions made by Carnine and his colleagues (1984), Jenkins and his colleagues (1984), Beck and McKeown (1991), Fukkink and de Glopper (1998), and Baumann and his colleagues (2005), only well-planned, powerful, and relatively lengthy instruction is likely to prove effective.

Word Parts. Considerations about teaching word parts can be conveniently grouped under three headings: What elements might we consider teaching? What elements do students know? And what are the effects of instruction about these elements? Here, I consider each of these in turn.

What Elements Might We Consider Teaching? Elements that might be considered include inflections, derivational suffixes, prefixes, and Latin and Greek roots. *Inflections* are suffixes that modify a base word changing aspects such as tense, number, aspect, and tense. Examples include the *-s* in *houses* and the *-ed* in *wanted*. They do not change the part of speech or the basic meaning of the word. *Derivational suffixes* are suffixes that modify root words, changing the part of speech and to some extent meaning. Examples include *-less* in *worthless* and *-able* in *adorable*. *Prefixes* are elements that are attached to the beginnings of words and change meaning. Examples include *un-* in *unhappy* and *re-* in *replay*. *Latin and Greek roots* are non-English word forms that are sometimes used as parts of English words. Examples include *tract* meaning "pull" as in *attract* and *extract* and *voc* meaning "call" as in *advocate* and *equivocate*.

What Elements Do Students Know? There is a good deal of research and wide agreement that children are competent in recognizing and using inflections well before entering school (Berko, 1958; Clark, 1993). The amount of research on children's competence with other elements is somewhat less.

With respect to derivational suffixes, Anglin (1993) found that first-grade children showed some but relatively little competence in recognizing derivational suffixes or in using them to infer the meanings of known root words to which the suffixes have been added. He also found that this competence increased for third-grade children and increased even more for fifth-grade children. Wysocki and Jenkins (1987) found that for fourth through eighth graders morphological generalization between suffixed and base words appeared in modest amounts when a strict criterion for knowing the related words was used but in much greater amounts when a weaker criterion was used. They further found that sixth and eighth graders displayed more morphological generalization that fourth graders. Freyd and Baron (1982) examined differences in knowledge of derived words between superior word learners in Grade 5 and average word learners in Grade 8 and found that the fifth-grade superior word learners showed more understanding of morphological generalization than the eighth-grade average word learners. Finally, Nagy, Diakidoy, and Anderson (1993) examined fourth-grade, seventh-grade, and high school students knowledge of the meanings of ten common derivational suffixes. Students' knowledge of the suffixes was found to undergo significant development between fourth grade and high school. Even in high school, however, some students showed little knowledge of the meanings of the suffixes tested. Note that none of these studies tell us just which derivational suffixes children know, just that they know some of them and this knowledge increases with age.

The data with respect to prefixes is more specific. O'Rourke (1974) tested sixth-grade students' knowledge of specific prefixes and found that the percentages of correct responses ranged from 10% for *dis-* to 37% for *re-*. Nicol (1980) tested fourth- through sixth-grade students and found that knowledge of prefix meanings ranged from 20% for *in-* meaning "not" to 88% for *mis-*. Finally, in the most telling study, White and his colleagues (White, Power, et al., 1989; White, Sowell, et al., 1989) identified the 20 most frequent prefixes in English and found that the top four of these prefixes (*un-, re-, in-* meaning "not", and *dis-*) accounted for 58% of the prefixed words in their sample. They then tested third- and fourth-grade students and found that three of these four prefixes were known by less than 50% of the students and the remaining prefix *un-* by just 63% of the students.

In one of very few studies to investigate students' knowledge of roots, Kaye and Sternberg (1983) found that eighth graders, tenth graders, and college undergraduates demonstrated some awareness of whether or not they knew a set of Latin roots and prefixes, but that only the college undergraduates appeared to decompose words into their component parts when determining the meanings of unknown words made up of the roots and prefixes. Note that this research did not investigate students' ability to perform the much easier task of decomposing words made up of a prefix and an English word. It appears to be the Latin roots, rather than the prefixes, that posed problems for secondary students.

Although lists of roots to teach are readily available (e.g., Dale, O'Rourke, & Bamman, 1971; Fry, 2004), I know of no reliable data on just which roots students know.

What Are the Effects of Instruction on Word Parts? Although not all studies aimed at teaching students word parts and the use of those word parts in unlocking the meanings of unknown words have produced positive results, some have definitely been successful. In one study, Heidi Hammond and I (Graves & Hammond, 1980) taught seventh graders the meanings of nine common prefixes and a strategy for using the prefixes to unlock the meanings of unknown words that contained the prefixes. Results indicated that the group taught the prefixes and the strategy outperformed a group simply taught whole words containing the prefixes and an uninstructed control group on a set of transfer words that contained the taught prefixes. In a follow-up study, Nicol, Graves, and Slater (1984) taught eight prefixes to fourth- through sixth-grade students in three 30-minute sessions. The instruction was similar to what Graves and Hammond used but provided more active involvement of students and more direct feedback by the teacher. Results on immediate and delayed transfer tests showed that the instructed students performed significantly better than an uninstructed control group. Results also indicated that high-, middle-, and low-ability students in all three grade levels benefited from the instruction.

In a study that involved both prefixes and suffixes, White, Sowell, and Yanagihara (1989) taught nine prefixes and a procedure for suffix removal twice weekly over a period of eight weeks. The instruction involved teacher-led active teaching with significant amounts of practice and feedback. Results indicated that instructed students outperformed uninstructed control students on a test identifying English base words by removing a suffix, a test identifying the meaning of the prefixed word when given the base word, and a test on the meanings of the prefixes.

The most recent studies of teaching word parts by Baumann and his associates (Baumann et al., 2003; Baumann et al., 2002) combined instruction in word parts with instruction in context clues and were partially described earlier in this chapter. In the 2002 study, one group, termed the morphemic-only group, was taught 20 prefixes in twelve 50-minute lessons. Another group, termed the morphemic-context group, was taught 20 prefixes and the use of context clues during this same amount of time. A third group received no special vocabulary instruction. Results indicated that students in the morphemic-only group and those in the morphemic-context group were more skillful in deriving the meaning of transfer words that contained the prefixes taught than students in the control group. In the 2003 study, students in some social studies classes were taught 20 prefixes and suffixes and the use of context clues, and students in the other classes were taught the key vocabulary from their social studies textbook. Results again indicated that the combined word-part and context-clue instruction was effective in teaching students to use word parts in unlocking the meanings of novel words and that the combined word-part and context-clue groups learned their social studies content as well as the students directly taught the social studies vocabulary.

In summary, the situation with word parts seems to be this: Children learn inflectional suffixes well before entering school and thus do not need to be taught them. First-grade children show little competence in recognizing derivational suffixes, and although competence increases with age, even some high school students show little knowledge of some of them. There is some evidence that derivational suffixes can be taught, and thus derivational suffixes are a reasonable target of instruction as students progress through school. Many upper elementary students do not know even the most common prefixes and there is good evidence that prefixes can and should be taught in the upper elementary grades. The situation with Latin and Greek roots is more problematic: There are hundreds of roots that might be taught; most roots are not used in a great many English words; the relationship between the original Greek or Latin meaning of a root and its meaning in and English word is vague; and roots are variously spelled, making them difficult for students to notice in words. For these reasons, it does not appear that systematic instruction in Greek and Latin roots should be a priority, at least below the secondary grades when roots become more common.

The Dictionary. Relevant studies here include investigations of what students understand from typical dictionary entries and investigations of how to improve dictionary entries.

In a study that is memorable because it revealed the extent to which students can misunderstand definitions, Miller and Gildea (1987) investigated the ability of fifth and sixth graders to generate appropriate sentences after reading traditional dictionary definitions. Results indicated that over 60% of the sentences students constructed were judged to be odd, often because students appeared to select only a fragment of the definition on which to base their sentence. For example, based on the dictionary definition of *eroding* that included the phrase "eating out," one student generated the sentence, "My family erodes a lot." Following this result, Miller and Gildea added example sentences to the definitions to see if that would improve performance. Results indicated that adding sentences seemed to improve students' performance but that improvement might have been artificial in that some of the correct sentences closely paralleled the sample sentences presented.

Scott and Nagy (1997) tested fourth-grade students on their understanding of definitions of verbs in two experiments. In the first experiment, students showed that they were quite proficient in distinguishing between correct definitions and totally incorrect definitions. However, neither less able nor more able students scored better than chance in identifying sentences that used a word with a meaning related to the definition but used it wrongly. In the second experiment, Scott and Nagy investigated the effects of modifying traditional definitions by using everyday English that clarified the subject and object of the verb being defined rather than the conventional format and by including an illustrative example sentence with fourth- and sixth-grade students. Results indicated that neither modification significantly affected students' performance, that sixth-grade students performed better than fourth-grade students, and that students with high verbal ability performed better than students with lower verbal ability. However, even the performance of high-ability sixth-grade students was far from perfect.

McKeown (1993) examined the effects of traditional definitions and definitions revised in a very systematic and principled way with fifth-grade students. For example, the traditional definition for *conspicuous* was "Easily seen," while the revised definition was "Describes something you notice right away because it stands out." Results of a task that required students to write sentences after reading traditional and revised definitions indicated that the traditional definitions yielded 25% acceptable sentences and 75% unacceptable sentences, while the revised sentences yielded 50% acceptable sentences and 50% unacceptable sentences. Another group of students received a different task, that of answering two questions about the meanings of words after receiving either a traditional definition or a revised definition. Results indicated that the revised definitions resulted in nearly three times as many correct responses and only half as many unacceptable responses. Additionally, surveys indicated that over 90% of the students and over 90% of a group of teachers preferred the revised definitions.

Finally, Nist and Olejnik (1995) presented college students with 10 nonsense words representing difficult nouns and both stronger and weaker definitions and measured their learning on four dependent measures. The measures were a typical multiple-choice item in which students chose a definition, a multiple-choice item in which students selected an example, a cloze item, and an item that required writing a sentence that clearly showed that students had learned the word's meaning. Students scored over 80% correct on the first three measures—recognition tasks—and 60% on the last measure—a fairly difficult production task. Results also indicated that students performed better with the stronger definitions on all four measures.

In summary, using the dictionary to define words is possible but difficult for elementary students and not 100% successful even for college students. Given these results, it appears that teaching students to more effectively use dictionaries to learn word meanings is useful throughout the elementary grades and in the secondary grades. It also appears that traditional dictionary entries need to be improved.

Fostering Word Consciousness

Word consciousness refers to a keen awareness of words and a keen interest in them. As Susan Watts and I have noted (Graves & Watts, 2002), "Students who are word conscious are aware of the words around them. This awareness involves an appreciation of the power of words, an understanding of why certain words are used in place of others, a sense of the words that could be used in place of those selected by a writer or speaker, and cognizance of first encounters with words" (p. 144). As my need to define the term suggests, word consciousness is a concept that has only recently been articulated. As a consequence, there is little research that directly demonstrates the effectiveness of word consciousness. Nevertheless, there are various sorts of evidence that strongly suggest its importance.

For one thing, leading vocabulary theorists and researchers including Anderson and Nagy (1992), Kame'enui and Baumann (2004), Beck, McKeown, and Kucan (2002), Blachowicz and Fisher (2004), Nagy (2005), and Scott and Nagy (2004) strongly support the inclusion of word consciousness as an integral and necessary part of an effective vocabulary program.

Another sort of evidence is the importance of motivation to all learning and for all students, from kindergartners (Pressley et al., 2003) to high school seniors (National Research Council, 2004). Students simply do not learn much unless they are motivated to do so, and if they are going to accomplish the huge task of learning something like 50,000 words by the time they graduate from high school, they absolutely must be motivated to do so.

Still another sort of evidence comes from a logical argument for the importance of metalinguistic awareness recently made by Nagy (in press). *Metalinguistic awareness* is the ability to recognize and reflect on various features of language, in this case features of words. It is one part of word consciousness. Students who have metalinguistic awareness of words recognize such features of words as their morphological makeup, their appropriateness in various contexts, and the way definitions function to define words. According to Nagy, a significant part of the relationship between vocabulary and reading comprehension may involve metalinguistic awareness, and some of the more powerful studies of vocabulary instruction may owe a large part of their success to fostering this type of word consciousness.

A final sort of evidence comes from vocabulary studies. In a series of relatively informal studies undertaken over a 7-year term, Scott and her colleagues (Scott, Butler, & Asselin, 1996; Scott & Nagy, 2004; Scott & Wells, 1998) investigated the effects of a project called The Gift of Words in which they provided students with an enriched focus on words in their reading, writing, and discussion. Results supported the effectiveness of this program on students' use of interesting words in their writing and on students' awareness and interest in words more generally. In another set of related studies, these by different researchers, word consciousness was an important part of multifaceted vocabulary programs designed to improve students' reading vocabulary and reading comprehension (Beck, McKeown, & Omanson, 1987), students' use of vocabulary in their writing (Duin & Graves, 1987), and English learners' general proficiency in vocabulary (Carlo et al., 2004). All of these programs produced strong positive results.

In summary, while word consciousness is a recently articulated concept and does not have an extensive research base, experts in the field and several studies strongly support including it as a significant component of the vocabulary curriculum.

Vocabulary Instruction for English Learners

For a number of years, vocabulary received relatively little attention in second language instruction, with grammar being the major focus (Folse, 2004; Long & Richards, 2001). Recently, however, that situation has changed, and vocabulary occupies an increasingly significant place in second-language theory and pedagogy (Carlo et al., 2004; Folse, 2004; Long & Richards, 2001; Nation, 2001; Schmitt, 2000). Clearly, vocabulary plays a major role in learning to read a second language. In fact, one study (Garcia, 1991) "found that unfamiliar English vocabulary was the major linguistic factor that adversely affected the Latina/o students reading test performance" (p. 822). Fortunately, much of the instruction appropriate for teaching vocabulary to native English speakers is appropriate for English-language learners (Fitzgerald, 1995; Slavin & Cheung, 2003). Still, there are some special needs that English learners have with respect to vocabulary and some special factors to consider.

1. *Students need to develop their oral language skills in both their native language and in English.* Research clearly shows that strong language skills in the native language facilitate students' reading in English (Slavin & Cheung, 2003), and that students make use of their skills in their first language to read in English (Jiménez, Garcia, & Pearson, 1996; Moll, 1988).

2. *Students need to develop a basic oral and reading vocabulary of the most frequent English words.* Second-language scholars agree that such a list comprises about 2,000 words (Cummins, 2003; Nation, 2001; Schmitt, 2000), and the most commonly recommended list is *A General Service List of English Words* (West, 1953). As Folse (2004) has noted, there are several other lists that can also be useful, and using a list does not necessarily mean simply teaching the words from the beginning of the list to the end. Teachers can use lists, for example, as clues to what words to teach and to what words probably do not need to be taught.

3. *Students need a vocabulary much larger than 2,000 words.* To succeed in school and after they leave school, students need a vocabulary of academic English (Cummins, 2003), a large vocabulary of words that are used in school texts and other readings for students and adults. Although native English speakers also need a vocabulary of academic English, learning it is likely to be easier for them, and many English learners need special attention in learning academic English. Note also that while much of the academic English vocabulary may represent new labels for known concepts for native English speakers, many of these same words will represent new concepts for English learners. As explained in Chapter 4, teaching new concepts requires more powerful instruction than does simply teaching new labels.

4. *Students need to master word-learning strategies—using context, using word parts, and using the dictionary.* Although native English speakers must also learn these strategies, word-learning strategies are particularly important for English learners because they have so many words to learn (Carlo et al., 2005). Additionally, the strategy of recognizing and using *cognates*—words that are similar in their native

language and in English—has been shown to be an important strategy for English learners (Garcia, 1991; Jiménez et al., 1996; Kamil & Hiebert, 2005; Nagy, Garcia, Durgunoglu, & Hancin-Bhatt, 1993).

Unfortunately, while theory and logic suggest some very reasonable approaches to vocabulary instruction for English learners, there is very little research on vocabulary instruction with these students. In fact, a review of reading programs for English learners completed in 2003 (Slavin & Cheung) included only two experimental studies of vocabulary instruction, and a yet-to-be published review by the National Literacy Panel on Language Minority Children and Youth includes only four experimental studies of vocabulary instruction since 1980 (D. August, personal communication, September 9, 2004).

In a small-scale and briefly reported study, Perez (1981) found that providing third-grade Mexican-American students with oral-language vocabulary enrichment activities for 20 minutes daily over a 3-month period, markedly increased their reading scores. In another small study, this one involving 42 bilingual, upper elementary, learning disabled children, Bos, Allen, and Scanlon (1989) compared the effects of teaching vocabulary using a definition method, a semantic mapping method, a semantic feature analysis method, or a method that coupled semantic feature analysis and cloze sentences. Results on a vocabulary measure indicated that students receiving the semantic feature analysis plus cloze instruction significantly outperformed students receiving the definition method. Results on a comprehension measure indicated that students in all other groups significantly outperformed students receiving the definition method. In a third small study Garcia (1996) found that after receiving individualized scaffolded instruction on using cognates, 10 of 13 fifth-grade Mexican-American students were able to use Spanish cognates to figure out unknown English words.

The fourth study is a large scale, ambitious, well-planned, and fully reported intervention by Carlo and her colleagues (2004). Over 250 fifth-grade students from nine classrooms in California, Massachusetts, and Virginia participated in the study. Students in the intervention classes were engaged in a 15-week, multifaceted program of vocabulary instruction. Students were taught the meanings of academic words, along with strategies for inferring word meanings using context, awareness of multiple meanings, morphology, and cognates. Principles underlying the instruction included the following: words should be encountered in meaningful contexts; students should see words in a variety of contexts; depth of meaning should be fostered; Spanish speakers should be able to access the texts' meaning in Spanish; and learning a word involves pronunciation, spelling, morphology, and syntax. Students in the intervention group showed larger gains than those in the control group on knowledge of the words taught, depth of knowledge, understanding multiple meanings, and reading comprehension. Additionally, an analysis of the data for students who participated in both the main study and a 10-week pilot study that preceded it showed that participating in the two interventions produced added benefits (Carlo et al., 2005). While not all instruction for English learners can include all of the components used in this study, the study bears close reading by anyone developing a vocabulary program for classrooms that include English learners, which means for most classrooms.

In summary, while there is relatively little research on vocabulary instruction for English learners, what research there is indicates that vocabulary instruction can produce gains in both vocabulary and comprehension, that instruction in cognates can help students figure out unknown words, and that rich and active instruction is useful for English learners just as it is for native English speakers.

CONCLUDING REMARKS

Given the difficulty of deciding just what will be counted as a word and what level of word knowledge should count as knowing a word, it is difficult to say exactly how many words students know or need to learn. However, there is good evidence to suggest that the texts and other reading materials students could encounter over 12–13 years of schooling contain over 180,000 word families; that average students learn to read something like 3,000–4,000 words each year; and that average students acquire reading vocabularies in the neighborhood of 50,000 words by the time they graduate from high school. To accomplish this very significant task, students need all the help that we can give them. There is also good evidence that linguistically disadvantaged students learn far fewer words and need even more assistance if they are to catch up with their peers.

Although the vocabulary instruction provided in schools has typically not been strong, it is improving. Moreover, there is a solid research base that can be used to further improve the vocabulary instruction students receive. Providing students with the assistance they need in building rich and powerful vocabularies means several things. First, it means ensuring that all students acquire a basic vocabulary of the most frequent words, a vocabulary of 1,000–3,000 words. While this is only a fraction of the words they must eventually learn, the 3,000 or so most frequent words account for approximately 75% of the words students will meet even in adult texts, and an even larger percentage of the words students will encounter in texts for the lower grades and in oral English. Second, it means teaching a number of words beyond these 1,000–3,000 most frequent words. For the most part, these will be important words from what students are reading, listening to, or otherwise studying in class. Third, it means teaching students word-learning strategies—using context, word parts, and the dictionary to glean word meanings. Powerful instruction is needed to teach these strategies. Fourth, it means making students word conscious, kindling their interest and enjoyment in words and furthering their metalinguistic awareness of words so that they become eager and knowledgeable word learners. Finally, while most of the assistance we provide for English learners will not be different in kind from that we provide for native English speakers, many English learners will need to be taught more words, will need more powerful instruction, and will need to be given particular help in mastering word-learning strategies.

CHAPTER 3

Providing Rich and Varied Language Experiences

You can't build a vocabulary without reading. You can't meet friends if you . . . stay at home by yourself all the time. In the same way, you can't build up a vocabulary if you never meet any new words. And to meet them you must read. The more you read the better. A book a week is good, a book every other day is better, a book a day is still better.

Rudolf Flesch and Abraham Lass, Professional Writers

This chapter has two major purposes. The first is to emphasize the fact that most words are learned incidentally, as students are reading, listening, talking, and writing. Given the size of the vocabularies that students eventually acquire—a receptive vocabulary of something like 50,000 words by the time they graduate from high school—only a small number of the words students learn can be directly taught. Thus, we need to do everything possible throughout students' 12–13 years of schooling to facilitate and encourage activities that will support incidental word learning.

The second purpose of the chapter is to stress that during the primary grades most of the new words children learn will come from listening and discussion, and to describe some powerful approaches to building vocabulary through listening and discussion. Instruction that builds vocabulary through listening and discussion activities is vitally important for primary-grade children who arrive at school with relatively small vocabularies. Primary-grade children will not learn many new words from the reading they do because the books they are able to read in kindergarten, first, and second grade are made up largely of words that are already in their oral vocabularies. Restricting the books children are learning to read to words that are already in their oral vocabularies makes good sense for beginning readers. The burden of learning the meanings of new words should not be added during the time that children are initially learning to read, to recognize the words on the printed page. However, not having the opportunity to learn new words is very unfortunate for children who enter school with small oral vocabularies; thus vocabulary instruction that goes beyond the words children encounter in the reading they do is essential.

PROMOTING INCIDENTAL WORD LEARNING

In the quotation that introduces this chapter, Flesch and Lass (1996) make a hugely important point. Children cannot build rich and powerful vocabularies without reading a great deal. In fact, over time, wide reading makes the single largest contribution to vocabulary development, much more than listening, discussion, or writing. When I first developed the four-part approach to vocabulary development described in this book, this part of the program was titled "Promoting Wide Reading." However, I have since changed that title because wide reading is not the only language experience students need to build rich and deep vocabularies. They also need to hear spoken language in a wide variety of situations and engage in frequent discussions in which they interact with other students, with teachers, and with other mature language users in real communicative situations. And they need to write a lot, for writing provides the opportunity and the incentive to really focus on words and choose just those words that will best convey their intended message to their intended audience. In the remainder of this section, I briefly discuss promoting incidental word learning through listening, reading, discussion, and writing.

Listening

In promoting students' incidental word learning through listening, your most powerful tool is the vocabulary you use in the classroom. Whatever grade level you teach, it is worthwhile making a deliberate effort to include some new and somewhat challenging words in your interactions with students. Selecting words to focus on or teach is no mean task, and it is a topic I discuss in some detail in Chapter 4. Briefly, however, by "new and somewhat challenging words," I generally mean what Beck and McKeown (2001) call "Tier 2 words." Tier 2 words are relatively high frequency words that are used by mature language users and that students are likely to encounter in the texts they read in upcoming years. Additionally, Tier 2 words are words that are used across domains—for example, in English, and history, and science—and not just in a single domain such as health or music. Of course, the Tier 2 words you want to introduce to students differ from one grade level to another. The ones to focus on are those that are not known by many students at that grade level and are thus a bit of a stretch. For primary-grade students, these might be words like *commotion, prowl,* and *timid.* For middle-grade students, they might be ones like *adjacent, exuberant,* and *ponder.* And for secondary students, they might be ones like *abstruse, extricate,* and *sophistry.* Note that at this point I am not talking about teaching these words, I am simply talking about using somewhat challenging words from time to time, sometimes pausing to explain their meanings but often just letting students hear them. For example, you might tell a group of seventh graders who have just come in from lunch and brought with them their cafeteria conversations that the *cacophony* they have brought in with them will not be needed that afternoon. The goal is to expose students to some new and challenging words and to peak their interest in such words.

Reading

In promoting students' incidental word learning through reading, considerations include recognizing the importance of wide reading, helping students select books that will promote vocabulary growth, and facilitating and encouraging their reading widely. Most words are learned from context, and the richest context for building vocabulary for students beyond the primary grades is books. Books, as Stahl and Stahl (2004) point out, are "where the words are." Testimony to that fact is shown in Figure 3.1. As can be seen in this chart listing the frequency of rare words, even children's books contain about one third more rare words than prime-time adult TV shows and nearly twice as many rare words as adult conversational speech.

If we want to help students increase their vocabularies, we need to get them to read more (Anderson, Wilson, & Fielding, 1988; Elley, 1996). Some reading, of course, can and should be done in class. I very strongly recommend some sort of in-class independent reading program in the elementary grades, particularly if the students are not avid readers. But there is only so much class time available. To really build their vocabularies, students need to read a lot outside of school. Unfortunately, both my informal conversations with teachers and students and the empirical evidence indicate that many children do very little reading outside of school (Anderson et al., 1988; National Assessment of Educational

Figure 3.1. Frequency of Rare Words in Various Sources

	Rare Words per 1,000
I. Printed texts	
Abstracts of scientific articles	128.0
Newspapers	68.3
Popular magazines	65.7
Adult books	52.7
Children's books	30.9
Preschool books	16.3
II. Television texts	
Prime time adult shows	22.7
Prime time children's shows	20.2
Mr. Rogers and *Sesame Street*	2.0
III. Adult speech	
Expert witness testimony	28.4
College graduates talk to friends/spouses	17.3

Note. Adapted from D. P. Hayes and M. Ahrens (1988), Vocabulary simplification for children: A special case of "motherese"? *Journal of Child Language, 15,* 395–410.

Progress, 2003). For example, in their study of how fifth-grade students spend their time out of school, Anderson and his colleagues (1988) found that 50% of the children read from books less than 4 minutes a day and 30% of the children read from books less than 2 minutes a day. Similarly, data gathered as part of the National Assessment of Educational Progress (2003) show that about one fourth of the students questioned reported reading no books outside of school in the previous month. These students, the ones who read no books outside of school or read books outside of school for only a few minutes a day, are almost certainly those most in need of larger vocabularies.

The starting point for encouraging wide reading is a well-stocked classroom library, a library with books that you know well, books appropriate for the various levels of readers in your classroom, and books that include appropriately challenging vocabulary. As Figure 3.1 suggests, newspapers and magazines are also valuable parts of the classroom library and are likely to contain the sort of challenging words students need to learn. While nothing can replace the immediacy and convenience of a classroom library, as children progress through elementary school and into the secondary grades, school and community libraries become increasingly important. Unfortunately, in poorer neighborhoods, classroom libraries, school libraries, and even community libraries are likely to have very meager resources (Neuman & Celano, 2001). Thus one task that teachers, schools, and communities face is doing everything possible to make books widely and conveniently available for students.

But just having books available is not enough—something must be done to entice children to read the books. Many possibilities exist here. Teachers of young children can read books aloud and then invite children to take the books home to reread. Teachers at all grade levels can read parts of books in class and encourage students to read the rest of the book at home, or they can give book talks that preview and advertise books the same way movie previews advertise upcoming films. They can encourage students to share the books they read with each other. They can become familiar with individual students' interests and with individual books and recommend particular books to particular students. They can require students to do some reasonable amount of reading outside of class. Some sort of in-class independent reading activity can be undertaken, particularly for students who, even with all of your efforts, are not likely to do much reading outside of school. Whether you call it DARE (Drop Everything and Read), SSR (Sustained Silent Reading), or USSR (Uninterrupted Sustained Silent Reading), some sort of ongoing, structured, long-term, in-school, silent reading program is a necessity for students who do not read outside of school.

Discussion

I turn now to promoting students' independent word learning through discussion. The key to having discussions that will prompt students to use more sophisticated vocabulary is to give them meaty and somewhat academic topics to talk about. As shown in Figure 3.1, casual conversations, even casual conversations among college graduates, do not include a lot of sophisticated vocabulary. If students are going to use sophisticated words, they need to discuss sophisticated ideas. This means talking about academic topics that students have some familiarity with—topics they are reading about, investigating in the library and on the Internet, and probably writing about. Such discussions might focus on science topics such as the ecology of fresh water lakes, social studies topics such as barriers to ordinary people running for public office, and sophisticated literary topics such as the motivations that prompt a character's action. One good source of meaty discussion topics is the literature on teaching for understanding, for example, Wiggins and McTighe's *Understanding by Design* (1998) or Wiske's *Teaching for Understanding* (1998).

Writing

The keys to promoting students' independent word learning through writing are similar to those for discussion. Students need to write about topics that they care about and that are at least somewhat sophisticated. They also need to write with a purpose and for an audience. This is the case because it is only when you are writing with a real purpose and for an audience that you have identified and care about that you are likely to ask the most important questions about the words you use in your writing: Here, for example, are some questions you might pose about words to middle and secondary school students:

- Does this word really capture my meaning?
- Is it the very best word to say just what I want to say?
- Will the people to whom I am writing understand this word?
- Will they find this word appropriately formal or informal as the situation demands?

Similar but simpler questions can be used with younger students. The goal is to get students to realize that the words they use in their writing are very important, that the words they use will affect both the clarity of what they write and the reaction their writing receives from others, and that therefore they should therefore choose and use words wisely, honing their word choices as one of the last steps in editing their writing.

DIRECTLY BUILDING PRIMARY GRADE CHILDREN'S ORAL VOCABULARIES

I turn now from the matter of indirectly building students' vocabulary by promoting incidental word learning—something that is necessary for all students at all grade levels—to directly building children's oral vocabularies—something necessary in the primary grades, particularly for children who enter school with small vocabularies. In kindergarten, most children can't read. And in first and second grade, they certainly do not read a lot. Moreover—and this is a major point and one that vocabulary scholars have only recently come to grips with—most of the books that primary grade children read themselves include relatively few words that are not already in their listening vocabularies

(Biemiller, 2004; McKeown & Beck, 2004). If children are going to learn really new words, words that are not already in their listening vocabularies, they are going to have to learn them through oral language activities. And the most powerful oral language activity that has been developed for use in classrooms is interactive oral reading.

Characteristics of Effective Approaches to Interactive Oral Reading

Over the past 30 years there have been a number of naturalistic studies of mothers reading to their preschool children. And over the past decade or so, there have been a number of experimental studies in which researchers, teachers, parents, and aides used specific procedures in reading to children with the goal of building their vocabularies, comprehension, and language skills more generally. Here, I call both the informal procedures mothers use and the more formal ones used in school *interactive oral reading*. The findings of studies on both sorts of interactive oral reading are highly consistent and serve to highlight the characteristics of effective approaches to building vocabulary in this way. On the following few pages, I discuss these characteristics and give some examples of them, drawing heavily on the work of De Temple and Snow (2003) as well as my own synthesis of the literature.

Effective Book Reading Is Interactive. Interactive reading means that both the reader and the children play active roles. The reader frequently pauses, prompts children to respond, and follows up those responses with answers and perhaps more prompts. Children respond to the prompts or questions, elaborate on some of their responses, and perhaps ask questions of their own. Additionally, the interactions are frequently supportive and instructive (Weizman & Snow, 2001). In other words, the reader scaffolds children's efforts to understand the words and the text, as illustrated in the following excerpt of a 5-year-old child and his mother reading Jill Murphy's *What Next, Baby Bear!*

> *Child:* I want to have ... what are those? Those are those are little little um volcanoes.
> *Mother:* Little *volcanoes.* Well yeah. Kind of. They're *craters.*
> *Child:* Craters?
> *Mother:* Yeah.
> *Child:* And the fire comes out of it?
> *Mother:* No. They just look like *volcanoes* but they're not.
> *Child:* Yeah, they're on the moon.
> *Mother:* Yeah. (Quoted in De Temple & Snow, 2003, p. 27)

Effective book reading usually involves reading the book several times. This allows the children and the reader to revisit the same topic and the same words several times, and it allows the children to begin actively using some of the words they have heard and perhaps had explained in previous readings.

Effective book reading directly focuses children's attention on a relatively small number of words. In some cases, the word work comes during the first reading, in some cases during subsequent readings, and in some cases after the book has been read.

Effective book reading requires the adult readers to read fluently, with appropriate intonation and with expression. Skilled adult readers effectively engage children with their animated and lively reading style.

Effective book reading requires carefully selected books. The books need to be interesting and enjoyable for children, and they need to stretch children's thinking a bit. Of course, the books also need to include some challenging words that are worth studying and will enhance children's vocabularies.

Effective book reading may involve nonimmediate talk interspersed with the oral reading. As defined by De Temple and Snow (2003), nonimmediate talk is "that talk produced by mother or child which goes beyond the information contained in the text or illustrations to make predictions, to make connections to the child's past experience, other books, or the real world; to draw inferences, analyze information, or discuss the meanings of words and offer explanations" (p. 21). Thus nonimmediate talk focuses on a number of factors, only one of which is vocabulary. But when it does focus on vocabulary, nonimmediate talk gives students opportunities to "understand and use the somewhat more sophisticated vocabulary required for evoking evaluative reactions to the book, discussing characters' internal states, making predictions concerning the next episode, and the like" (p. 21).

The following excerpt from a mother reading to her 6-year-old son from an expository book on elephants (Mary Hoffman's *Animals in the Wild*) shows how the reader is able to discuss a topic very remote from the family's day-to-day experience and introduce several words related to the topic.

Mother: That's a tusk see. It's white. Know what Domingo?
Child: Hmm.

Mother: Hunters kills these elephants for that.

Child: Why?

Mother: Because they want it for, um, well, they use it for different things I think um some musicians buy them and I don't know about museums but I know that they kill them for this white um.

Child: There's no tusks on these elephants though.

Mother: See. That one's bigger so some of them die because of that. That is sad.

Child: I wish there was not such things as hunters and guns.

Mother: I know it. Me too. Oh there's a herd. That's a lot of them. See how they walk?

Child: Ma here's ones that's dead.

Mother: I don't think he's dead! Well, we'll find out. "They use their tusks to dig." Oh see he's digging a hole! "They use their tusks to dig for salt. . . ."

Child: Hmm.

Mother: Let's look and see if there's another page you might like. It's ivory! The tusks are made of ivory. And they can make things with these tusks and that's why some animals, they die, humans kill them.

Child: No wonder why, they have hunters.

Mother: Yeah that's sad.

Child: I never gonna be a hunter when I grow up.

Mother: Oh thank God I'm glad. (Quoted in De Temple & Snow, 2003, pp. 23–24)

As I cautioned in introducing the concept of nonimmediate talk, effective book reading *may* involve nonimmediate talk. I say *may* for several reasons. Some evidence (Reese & Cox, 1999) indicates that with younger children more direct attention to the text may be more fruitful. In some cultures, reading to students typically involves more direct attention to the text (De Temple & Snow, 2003). Some authorities (e.g., Beck & McKeown, 2001) believe strongly that attending to the meaning of the text ought to be the top priority. Additionally, there is always the concern that paying too little attention to the text during oral reading can give children the false impression that texts are simply prompts or jumping-off points for wide-ranging thoughts and discussions and that there is no need to pay close attention to the text itself. Thus deciding how discursive to be during interactive book reading is a judgment that adult readers will need to make on a case-by-case basis.

Four Research-Based Programs for Interactive Oral Reading

Having considered the general characteristics of effective approaches to building vocabulary through oral reading, I turn now to describing four programs that have been shown to be effective and that can be used as models for a program in your school. The first of these is Whitehurst's *Dialogic Reading.* Dialogic Reading is a one-to-one interactive picture-book reading approach designed for preschool children. Studies have shown that parents, teachers, and aides can use the approach to produce gains in the vocabulary and language development of preschool children. The second program is Biemiller's approach, which I have termed *Direct and Systematic Instruction.* Direct and Systematic Instruction is an interactive book reading approach designed to foster vocabulary growth in kindergarten through second-grade children. Several studies have demonstrated the effectiveness of the approach and led to refined and more powerful versions of it. The third program is Beck and McKeown's *Text Talk.* Text Talk is an interactive book reading approach designed to foster comprehension and vocabulary growth in kindergarten through second-grade children. A recent study has shown that teachers can use the procedure to teach young children sophisticated words. The last program I discuss here is Juel and Deffes's *Anchored Instruction.* Anchored Instruction is an approach that simultaneously deals with word meanings, sounds, and spelling. A recent study has shown that this multifaceted approach is more powerful than simpler ones.

Dialogic Reading. As noted, Dialogic Reading (Whitehurst et al., 1988; Whitehurst et al., 1994; Zevenbergen & Whitehurst, 2003) is a one-to-one picture-book interactive reading technique designed for preschoolers. It can be used by teachers, teacher aids, other caregivers, and parents to foster vocabulary development and language development more generally. Like other interactive oral reading techniques, Dialogic Reading begins with the understanding that there are more and less effective ways to orally share books with children, and that a carefully designed procedure can maximize the effectiveness of oral reading. The procedure is "based on the theory that practice in using language, feedback regarding language, and appropriately scaffolded adult-child interactions in the context of picture-book reading all facilitate young children's language development" (Zevenbergen & Whitehurst, 2003). Two sets of procedures have been developed, one for 2–3-year-olds and one for 4–5-year-olds. Both procedures encourage the child to become the teller of the story over time, prompt the child by using questions, expand the child's vocabularies by highlighting words that are likely to be new to the child, and praise the child for her efforts in telling the story and labeling objects depicted in the book. Additionally, consistent with Vygotsky's (1978) principle of the zone of proximal development, over time the adult continually nudges the child toward more sophisticated language and thinking than she would be likely to use on her own.

The dialogic reading procedure for 4–5-year-olds recommends that adult readers elicit children's responses using the five types of prompts shown in the list that follows.

Prompts Used with Dialogic Reading

1. *Completion prompts*: Fill-in-the-blank questions (e.g., "When we went into the car, we all put our. . . .")
2. *Recall prompts*: Questions that require the child to remember aspects of the book (e.g., "Can you remember some of the things that Sticky-beak did at school?")
3. *Open-ended prompts*: Statements that encourage the child to respond to the book in her own terms (e.g., "Now it's your turn to tell about this page.")
4. *Wh-prompts*: What, where, and why questions (e.g., "What is this called?" "Why did Peter stay home from school?")
5. *Distancing prompts*: Questions that require the child to relate the content of the book to aspects of life outside of school (e.g., "Did we ever go to a parade like Susan did?") (Zevenbergen & Whitehurst, 2003, p. 180)

The approach also includes the four procedures listed below.

Procedures Used with Dialogic Reading

1. *Prompt.* Ask the child to label objects in the pictures and talk about the story (e.g., pointing to a picture, "What do you call this?" "Why do you think the puppy looks sad?")
2. *Evaluate.* Praise the child's correct answers and offer alternate labels or correct answers for incorrect responses (e.g., "Very good. That *is* a duck." "No, that's not a chicken, it's a duck.")
3. *Expand.* Repeat what the child said and add information not in the child's response (e.g., "Yes, the puppy does look sad. I think that's because he doesn't have a home. Do you think that would make him sad?")
4. *Repeat.* Guide the child to repeat the expanded response (e.g., "Can you tell me why the puppy might look sad?")

Each instance of dialogic reading is of course somewhat different, but the following parent-child dialogue about Ezra Jack Keats's *The Snowy Day* is a good example of the procedure.

Parent: "The Snowy Day." What's he doing here?

Child: Sliding.

Parent: Yeah. He's sliding down a hill. Can you say that?

Child: He's sliding down a hill.

Parent: Good. "One winter morning Peter woke up and looked out the window. Snow had fallen during the night. It covered everything as far as he could see." What does he see outside his window?

Child: Snow.

Parent: That's right. There's lots of snow outside.

Child: Yeah.

Parent: "After breakfast he put on his snowsuit and ran outside. The snow was piled up very high along the street to make a path for walking." Your turn. What's happening on this page?

Child: He is making steps in the snow.

Parent: That's right. He's making footprints.

Child: Footprints.

Parent: Do you remember when we played outside in the snow?

Child: Yeah. And we made snowballs.

Parent: You remember. We made a lot of snowballs. I remember that you made footprints all around the yard too.

Child: Yeah.

Parent: "Then he dragged his feet s-l-o-w-l-y to make tracks. And he found something sticking out of the snow that made a new track." What do you think it was that made a new track?

Child: A dog?

Parent: Well, it looks like it might be something else that makes the track. Let's see what it is next. "It was a . . . ."

Child: Stick.

Parent: Yes. "It was a stick—a stick that was right for smacking a snow-covered . . . ."

Child: Tree.

Parent: Okay. What happens next?

Child: He got snow on his head.

Parent: That's right. (Zevenbergen & Whitehurst, 2003, pp. 195–196)

There are two video tapes designed to train parents and teachers to use Dialogic Reading (*Read Together, Talk Together: Parent Video,* 2002; *Read Together, Talk Together: Teacher Training Video,* 2002). Research has shown that these tapes can effectively train parents, teachers, and teachers aids to use the approach (Arnold, Lonigan, Whitehurst, & Epstein, 1994).

Direct and Systematic Instruction. As noted, Direct and Systematic Instruction (Biemiller, 2001, 2003) is an interactive oral reading technique intended for kindergarten through second-grade children. As the name suggests, the procedure includes some very direct instruction, more direct than that provided in some of the other approaches. Also, Direct and Systematic Instruction differs from some of the other programs in that vocabulary development is the sole concern. The procedure is directly motivated by the fact that the vocabularies of disadvantaged children lag well behind those of their more advantaged peers and that the instruction needed to make up that gap needs to be "early, direct, and sequential" (Biemiller, 2001).

The first step is to select books. The program uses one book per week, and in order to teach the number of words necessary to markedly increase disadvantaged students' vocabularies the program should be used for at least 1 year and preferably for 3 years. About 30 books are needed for each year. As it has usually been implemented, the approach uses narratives. Typical of books appropriate for kindergarten are Norman Birdwell's *Clifford at the Circus* and Phoebe Gillman's *Jillian Jiggs*. Typical of those appropriate for Grade 1 are Alice Schertle's *Down the Road* and Dayal Khalsa's *Julian*. And typical of those appropriate for Grade 2 are Leo Lionni's *Alexander and the Windup Mouse*, and Stephanie McLellan's *The Chicken Cat*.

The next step, and one that is given more attention in Biemiller's approach (see particularly Biemiller, 2005) than in other interactive oral reading approaches, is selecting words. Unfortunately, in this program as in the others, selecting words "remains an art, not a science" (Biemiller & Boote, 2004). Words are selected based on the teacher's intuition that they (1) are known by some but not all children at that grade level and (2) are not rare or obscure words and thus are likely to be useful to children as they progress into the upper elementary grades. Although deciding just how difficult the words should be remains a matter of intuition, there are several sources you can check to avoid including words that are likely to be known by most children. The words on Dale's list of 3,000 words (Chall & Dale, 1995)—words that Dale found that 80% of fourth-grade students he tested knew—are probably too easy and should not be used to build students' oral vocabularies. Some samples of words that have been used with the procedure and the percentages of students Biemiller and Boote (2004) reported as knowing the words prior to instruction are shown in Figure 3.2.

Two important characteristics of these words should be noted. First, they are not rare and obscure words. They are words that children are likely to hear or use themselves in speaking, and they are words that they are likely to find in the books they read in the elementary years. Second, they span a range of difficulty. Since this is a whole-class procedure, the goal is to include some words that will be a challenge for most of the children and some that will be a challenge for only some children.

Figure 3.2. Sample of Words Used with Direct and Systematic Instruction with Percentages of Students Knowing Them

Kindergarten	First Grade	Second Grade
slip (8%)	snag (4%)	envy (3%)
obey (16%)	chance (11%)	scowl (12%)
coop (22%)	certainly (29%)	glance (26%)
parade (34%)	realize (45%)	restless (40%)
fairy (57%)	pile (72%)	appetite (50%)

Select about 24 words from each book. Students will not remember all the words that are taught, but Biemiller estimates that if this number of words were taught each week over a school year, children might learn 400 words. Although children with the smallest vocabularies will not catch up with those with larger vocabularies, knowing 400 more words is a significant improvement.

The third step is to implement the procedure over 5 days as shown in the outline.

Teaching Procedure for Direct and Systematic Instruction

- *Day 1.* Read the book through once including some comprehension questions after reading it but not interrupting the reading with vocabulary instruction. [Experience has shown that children may object to interrupting the first reading of the book with vocabulary instruction.]
- *Day 2.* Reread the book, teaching about eight words. When you come to a sentence containing a target word, stop and reread the sentence.

  After rereading the word, give a brief explanation. For example, after reading the sentence "It seemed like a good *solution*" in a second-grade book, pose the question "What does solution mean?" Then, answer your question with something like "A solution is the answer to a problem." Remember to keep the definitions simple, direct, and focused on the meaning of the word as it was used in the story.

  At the end of the day's instruction, review the words taught by rereading the sentences in which they appeared and the definitions you gave.

- *Days 3 and 4.* Reread the story two more times, teaching about eight new words each time. As on Day 2, briefly define the words as you come to them and review all of them at the end of the reading.
- *Day 5.* At the end of the week, review all of the words taught that week, this time using sentences to provide some variety but giving the same definitions.

Used in this way, the procedure will require about half an hour a day and will result in students learning a significant number of words over the course of a year. Of course, if the procedure is used from kindergarten through second grade—and this is Biemiller's goal—an even more significant number of words will be learned.

Text Talk. As noted, Text Talk (Beck & McKeown, 2001; McKeown & Beck, 2003) is an interactive book reading procedure designed to foster comprehension and develop vocabulary in kindergarten through second-grade children. Unlike Dialogic Reading and Direct and Systematic Instruction, Text Talk focuses on more sophisticated vocabulary, beginning with a focus on comprehension and dealing with vocabulary only after the complete book has been read and discussed. As with the other interactive oral reading procedures, Text Talk emphasizes the importance of the talk surrounding the text, the active involvement of students, asking open-ended questions, and gradually turning over increased responsibility to students.

The texts used are narratives, specifically selected to include an event structure and some complexities that will be worthy of discussion. As the teacher reads the story, she intersperses open-ended questions that require students to describe and explain ideas in the text rather than simply recall what happened. Based on the students' initial responses, the teacher asks follow-up questions that encourage students to elaborate and further develop their initial ideas. Pictures are generally presented after children have listened to and discussed a section of the text, so that the focus is on understanding text rather than responding to pictures. In a departure from the emphasis on nonimmediate talk emphasized in some interactive oral reading approaches, background knowledge is dealt with judiciously and used to support students building meaning from the text rather than to consider tangential experiences. Finally, as mentioned above, vocabulary is dealt with only after the story has been completed.

The vocabulary instruction itself focuses on two to four words from the story. These are selected because they are likely to be new words for the children, represent available concepts, are likely to be used by mature language users, and are somewhat sophisticated words. Some examples of the sort of words used are shown in Figure 3.3. As can be seen, while these are not rare or obscure words, they are sophisticated ones. Focusing on sophisticated words is a deliberate choice Beck and McKeown make. Many of the students in kindergarten and first grade would find them unfamiliar.

A typical lesson begins with a description of how the word is used in the story. Then the teacher explains the word's meaning and describes a situation in which it might be used. Next, the teacher prompts students to respond to the word in some way that requires them to actively consider its meaning; for example, she might use the word in a sentence and ask students to judge whether or not she has used it correctly. Here is an example of how the word *reluctant*, which appears in Don Freeman's *A Pocket for Corduroy*, would be presented.

Sample Text Talk Presentation

- First, the word is contextualized for its role in the story. (In the story, Lisa was reluctant to leave the laundromat without Corduroy.)
- Next, the meaning of the word is explained. (*Reluctant* means you are not sure you want to do something.)
- The children are asked to repeat the word so that they can create a phonological representation of the word. (Say the word with me: *reluctant*.)
- Examples in contexts other than the one used in the story are provided. (Someone might be reluctant to eat a food that they never had before, or someone might be reluctant to ride a roller coaster because it looks scary.)

Figure 3.3. Sample of Words Used with Text Talk

Kindergarten	First Grade
disappear	immense
annoy	astonished
timid	clutching
enormous	snarl
sprout	radiant

- Children make judgments about examples (Which would you be reluctant to hold: a kitten or a rattlesnake? Why?)
- Children construct their own examples (Think about something that you would be reluctant to do. Start your sentence with "I would be reluctant to. . . .")
- The word's phonological and meaning representation are reinforced. (What's the word that means not wanting to do something?) (Beck, McKeown, & Kucan, 2002, pp. 51–52)

In addition to introducing the words in this way, teachers using the procedure reinforce children's learning with a variety of activities in the days and weeks following the initial instruction. For example, they post charts of the words, keep tallies of when they come up in class discussions or reading, and use them in ongoing class activities such as the morning message. All in all, children should have a good deal of active experience with the words.

In addition to the basic Text Talk procedure, which is itself quite robust, Beck and McKeown have also developed and tested an Extended Text Talk procedure. Here, the initial instruction is the same as in the regular Text Talk except that there is more of it, with initial instruction on the words extending over 4 days rather than 1 day and with two review cycles added. In all, the Extended Text Talk involves about four times as much instruction as the basic version. A formal experiment has shown that both sorts of instruction result in significant gains, but that the gains from the Extended Text Talk are about twice as large as those from the basic version (Beck & McKeown, 2004). This is a substantial gain. At the same time, it comes at a very substantial cost: four times as much instruction. My suggestion is to try the basic version first, then try the extended version, and decide for yourself whether or not the extended time is worth it.

Anchored Instruction. Anchored Instruction is a vocabulary teaching technique to use with read-alouds for kindergarten and first-grade children (Juel & Deffes, 2004). It is motivated by two primary considerations. First, while it is important to focus on decoding skills in the first years of school, this does not mean that we should assume that children know the meanings of all of the words they will encounter during storybook reading. Such relatively common words as *hog, thorn,* and *pond* have been shown to be unfamiliar to some primary-grade students (Juel & Deffes, 2004). Thus, as you are reading through stories and choosing words to use in building decoding skills, you also want to be on the lookout for words whose meanings students may not know. The second argument motivating

Anchored Instruction is that thoroughly teaching words, teaching them in such a way that students really learn them and remember them over time, will be facilitated if instruction is multifaceted.

Anchored Instruction is multifaceted in that it deals with the context in which the word occurs, the word's meaning, some aspect of decoding, and spelling. Dealing with these multiple aspects of the word gives students multiple memory hooks they can use in storing and retrieving the words. The procedure includes the four steps shown in the list that follows.

Procedure Used with Anchored Instruction

- Use the procedure with books that are interesting to students and at an appropriate level for a read-aloud, yet include some potentially useful words that at least some students may not know.
- Identify several words to teach for a particular book, and make individual word cards for each student.
- Plan instruction in which you relate the words to students' background knowledge, define them (a step I have added), and call students' attention to some of the component letters and sounds.
- Read the book aloud, pausing for instruction as you come to each word.

Here's an example in which the teacher works at the same time with the words *quarreled* and *quibbled*, which came up in the sentence "They quarreled and quibbled from dawn to dusk" in Leo Lionne's *It's Mine*. A substantial amount of attention is given to letter-sound correspondences and to spelling, making the procedure very different from the other interactive oral reading procedures considered in this chapter.

Sample Anchored Instruction Lesson

Teacher: In the beginning, the book said the frogs were *quarreling* and *quibbling*. What did they do? Were they friends or enemies at the beginning? If you quarrel with a friend, what would you feel like? What would quibbling sound like? Show me.

[*Students respond.*]

Teacher: That's right, both *quarrel* and *quibble* mean about the same thing. They mean "to argue," and *quibble* usually means to argue over something that is not very important. [This step was not in Juel & Deffes.]

Teacher: Find the cards for *quarrel* and *quibble*. [Students have their own word cards.] This word is *quarrel* and this word is *quibble*. [The teacher uses word cards in a pocket chart to model.] They look a lot alike, and they mean similar things. What sound is at the beginning of *quarrel*? Two letters make that one sound. Point to those two letters. What letters are they? What sound is at the beginning of *quibble*? Two letters make that one sound. Point to those two letters. Are those the same letters as in *quarrel*? Does *qu* have the same sound in *quarrel* and in *quibble*?

[*Students respond.*]

Teacher: Let's look at *quarrel*. Show me your cards. What sound is in the middle of "quar-r-r-rel"? What letter is that? Point to that letter. What sound do you hear at the end of "quarrel-l-l-l-l"? What letter is that? Point to that letter.

[*Students respond.*]

Teacher: Now let's look at *quibble*. Show me your cards. What sound is in the middle of "quib-b-b-ble"? What letter is that. Point to that letter. What sound do you hear at the end of "quibbl-l-l-l-le"? What letter is that? There is a silent *e* that doesn't make any sound after that letter. Point to the letter that says /l/. How are *quarrel* and *quibble* alike? How are they different? (Juel & Deffes, 2004, p. 33)

In addition to including attention to meaning, sound, and spelling, Anchored Instruction has two additional notable features: (1) It is very explicit and very detailed; the teacher knows exactly what she wants the children to do and to learn. (2) It includes a lot of active responding and thought on the part of the child. Of course, you also need to decide how much of the procedure to devote to decoding and spelling rather than meaning. All three are important, but including all three comes at a definite cost in terms of time. If less were done with sound and spelling, then more could be done with meaning, or more words could be dealt with. It is a matter of deciding what is most beneficial for students.

Word Consciousness Activities for the Primary Grades

Given the large vocabulary deficits that many less advantaged children face, direct attempts to build their vocabularies with procedures like Dialogic Reading, Direct and Systematic Instruction, Text Talk, and Anchored Instruction make good sense. At the same time, it is important to recognize that such approaches can do only some of the work necessary to narrow the vocabulary gap between less advantaged and more advantaged children. Other approaches—approaches that permeate the school day and school year, extend into students' lives outside of school, and get students interested in words and excited about them—are an absolute necessity. The goals of such activities are to make students consciously aware of the words they and others use and to encourage them to really value words. In Chapter 6, I describe word consciousness activities for all grade levels. Here, I want to give just one example of a word consciousness activity particularly appropriate for primary-grade children as a reminder of the absolute necessity of such activities. This activity, a particular version of the widely used word-of-the-day approach, was developed by Katch (2004), who teaches 4-, 5-, and 6-year olds.

Shortly before beginning the activity, establish the concept of "special words," words for things that children love, would really like to have, or perhaps even fear: *Christmas, kitty, daddy,* and *ghost* are examples. Also before beginning the activity, put each child's name on a card and tack the cards on a corkboard so that each child has a column for her words.

Each day, have one child bring in her special word, put it in her column on the corkboard, read it, talk about what makes it special, and read each of the special words that other children have brought in. After one row is completed, children start a second row, again reading the words they contribute as well as other children's words until there are too many words to read every day. At that point, the child who brings in a word for the day reads all of her words but only one of the rows of other children's words.

As the school year progresses, make it a point to highlight individual words over time, perhaps mentioning whose word it is and its special meaning or perhaps using the word to review some aspect of letter-sound correspondences. Part of the goal is to feature and celebrate these special words—"The Most Important Words," as they are referred to in the title of Katch's (2004) article. Another part of the goal is to highlight, celebrate, and kindle children's interest in words generally.

CONCLUDING REMARKS

Providing rich and varied language experiences—experiences in reading, writing, listening, and discussing—is vitally important. This is something we need to do for all students at all age and grade levels and all levels of proficiency. Students can only develop rich and powerful vocabularies if they engage in many and varied activities that invite, motivate, and prompt them to learn and use sophisticated and appropriate words. Providing special help for primary-grade children who enter school with relatively small vocabularies—including English learners with small English vocabularies—is also vitally important. Interactive oral reading activities such as Dialogic Reading, Direct and Systematic Instruction, Text Talk, and Anchored Instruction are the most thoroughly researched and theoretically sound ways of doing that. Adding a focus on word consciousness to these more formal approaches will further promote vocabulary growth and make the classroom a more lively and interesting place for children and teachers alike, and requires very little classroom time or preparation. Together, these approaches will go a long way toward enriching the vocabularies of all children.

CHAPTER 4

Teaching Individual Words

Consider the power that a name gives a child. Now this is a *table* and
that a *chair*. . . . Having a name for something means that one has some
degree of control. . . . As children get more words, they get more
control over their environment. . . . Language and reading both act as the
tools of thought to bring representation to a new level and to allow
the formation of new relationships and organizations. . . . To expand a
child's vocabulary is to teach that child to think about the world.
Steven Stahl and Katherine Dougherty Stahl, Vocabulary Scholars

As Stahl and Stahl (2004) so eloquently note, having a name for
something gives children a tremendous advantage. As children's
vocabularies grow, so do their abilities to think about their
world, to exercise some control over it, and, of course, to communicate
their thoughts to others. As I noted in earlier chapters and will again
note in this one, over their years of schooling students are faced with
learning a truly astounding number of words, many more that we could
possibly teach one by one. However, the fact that students need to learn
more words than we can possibly teach them does not mean that we
should not teach them some words. In fact, we should teach them a lot
of words.

Teaching individual words pays a number of important dividends.
First, and most obviously, teaching a child a word leaves him with one
less word to learn independently. Second, teaching individual words
gives students a store of words that they can use to explore and understand their environment. Third, teaching individual words can increase
students' comprehension of selections containing those words. Fourth,
teaching individual words can increase the power and overall quality
of students' oral and written communications skills. Finally, and very
importantly, teaching individual words demonstrates our interest in
words, and teaching them in engaging and interesting ways fosters
students' interest in words.

In this chapter, I discuss a number of effective ways to teach individual words. Using different ways of teaching individual words is important for several reasons. For one thing, different words represent different learning tasks. For example, some of the words you teach will be words that are in students' listening vocabularies but that they don't recognize in print, while others will be words that are not in students' listening vocabularies and represent new and difficult concepts. For another thing, in different situations you will have different goals for teaching a word. In one case, for example, you may just want to introduce the word so that students won't stumble over it when they see it in an upcoming passage. In another, you will want to give students deep, rich, and lasting meanings for a word. Yet another reason for using different ways of teaching words is that some students will learn best with and prefer some methods while other students will learn best with and prefer other methods. And yet one more reason for using different methods is to provide some variety for both students and yourself. If each and every time you taught vocabulary you taught it in just the same way, both you and your students would soon tire of the approach.

This chapter is divided into three parts. In the first part, I discuss several factors that need to be considered before you actually teach words, including the various learning tasks that different words represent. In the second and much longer part, I describe and give examples of instructional methods for accomplishing the various word-learning tasks. In the third part, I discuss how to select a method, including which methods would likely improve reading comprehension.

PRELIMINARY CONSIDERATIONS

In this section, a precursor to the discussion of specific procedures for teaching individual words, I discuss five topics that influence the decisions that must be made about teaching words: how many words students need to learn over the elementary and secondary school years; levels of word knowledge; various word-learning tasks that students face with different words; some ways of determining which words to teach and which not to teach; and some general principles of vocabulary instruction.

How Many Words Must Students Learn?

Most students enter school with relatively large oral vocabularies—perhaps 10,000 words—and quite small reading vocabularies—perhaps numbering only a few words. As I explained in some detail in Chapter 2, ahead of them lies a sizable task. The work of Anderson and Nagy (1992), Anglin (1993), Miller and Wakefield (1993), Nagy and Anderson (1984), Nagy and Herman (1987), and White, Graves, and Slater (1990) suggests that students learn from 3,000 to 4,000 word families each year and can read something like 50,000 words by the time they graduate from high school.

Obviously, students learn many more words each year than we can teach directly. Teaching the 3,000 to 4,000 or so words that students learn each year during a typical 180-day school year would mean teaching something like 20 words a day. This does not, should not, and could not happen. However, as I have noted, the fact that we cannot directly teach all of the words students need to learn does not mean that we cannot and should not teach some of them. Moreover, the figures I have given here are for average students. As I explained in Chapter 2, linguistically disadvantaged students and English learners may have much smaller vocabularies, making teaching individual words even more important for them.

Levels of Word Knowledge

Another factor to consider in teaching individual words is the level of word knowledge that students need to achieve. As noted in Chapter 2, word knowledge exists on a continuum ranging from absolutely no knowledge of the word to rich and powerful knowledge of the word. Here, again, is the continuum Beck, McKeown, and Kucan (2002) have suggested.

- No knowledge
- General sense, such as knowing *mendacious* has a negative connotation
- Narrow, context-bound knowledge, such as knowing that a *radiant* bride is a beautifully smiling happy one, but unable to describe an individual in a different context as radiant
- Having knowledge of a word but not being able to recall it readily enough to apply it in appropriate situations
- Rich, decontextualized knowledge of a word's meaning, its relationship to other words, and its extension to metaphorical uses, such as understanding what someone is doing when they are *devouring* a book (p. 10)

Certainly, no single encounter with a word is likely to produce all of these types of knowledge. On the other hand—and this is a critical point underlying the task of teaching individual words—no single encounter with a word needs to produce all of these types of knowledge.

Instead, any particular encounter with a word can be considered as only one in a series of experiences that will eventually lead students to mastery of the word. Even a brief encounter with a word will leave some trace of its meaning and make students likely to more fully grasp its meaning when they again come across it. Moreover, brief instruction provided immediately before students read a selection containing the word may be sufficient to prevent their stumbling over it as they read.

Thus the methods described in this chapter include relatively brief instruction that serve primarily to start students on the long road to full mastery of words, as well as more time consuming, extensive, and ambitious instruction that enables students to develop thorough understandings of words and perhaps use the words in their speech and writing. It is important to recognize that, while students need not learn all words thoroughly, they must learn most words they will encounter frequently in reading well enough that their responses to them are automatic, that is, instantaneous and without attention (LaBerge & Samuels, 1974). Otherwise, the need to shift from attention to larger units of meaning—clauses, sentences, and entire passages—to individual words will overload memory limitations and thwart the meaning–getting process.

The Word-Learning Tasks Students Face

As I have repeatedly noted, all word-learning tasks are not the same. Word-learning tasks differ depending on such matters as how much students already know about the words to be taught, how well you want them to learn the words, and what you want them to be able to do with the words afterwards. Here, I consider eight tasks students face in learning words, some of which are quite different from others and require quite different sorts of instruction.

Learning a Basic Oral Vocabulary. As noted, many children arrive at school with substantial oral vocabularies, perhaps numbering 10,000 words. However, some linguistically disadvantaged children come to school with meager oral vocabularies, and some English learners come to school with even more limited English vocabularies. For such children, building a basic oral vocabulary of the most frequent English words is of utmost importance. Because learning a basic oral vocabulary is so important, I discussed it at length in a separate chapter, Chapter 3. It will not be considered further in this chapter.

Learning to Read Known Words. Learning to read known words—words that are already in their oral vocabularies—is the major vocabulary learning task of beginning readers. Such words as *surprise, stretch*, and *amaze* are ones that students might be taught to read during their first three years of school. By third or fourth grade, good readers will have learned to read most of the words in their oral vocabularies. However, the task of learning to read many of the words in their oral vocabularies remains for many less proficient readers and for some English learners.

Learning New Words Representing Known Concepts. A third word-learning task students face is learning to read words that are in neither their oral nor their reading vocabularies but for which they have an available concept. For example, the word *goulash* meaning a type of stew would be unknown to a number of third graders. Similarly, the word *ensemble* meaning a group of musicians would be an unknown word for many ninth graders. But in both cases the concepts are familiar. All students continue to learn words of this sort throughout their years in school, making this one of the major word-learning tasks students face. It is also a major learning task for English learners, who, of course, have a number of concepts for which they do not have English words.

Learning New Words Representing New Concepts. Another word-learning task students face, and a very demanding one, is learning to read words that are in neither their oral nor their reading vocabularies and for which they do not have an available concept. Learning the full meanings of such words as *equation, impeach*, and *mammal* is likely to require most elementary students to develop new concepts, while learning the full meanings of such words as *mass, enzyme*, and *fascist* will require most high school students to develop new concepts. All students continue to learn words of this sort throughout their years in school and beyond. Once again, learning new concepts will be particularly important for English learners. Also, students whose backgrounds differ from that of the majority culture will have internalized a set of concepts that is at least somewhat different than the set internalized by students in the majority culture. Thus words that represent known concepts for some groups of students will represent unknown concepts for other groups.

Learning New Meanings for Known Words. Still another word-learning task is learning new meanings for words that students already know with one meaning. Many words have multiple meanings, and thus students frequently encounter words that look familiar but are used with a meaning different from the one they know. Students will encounter such words throughout the elementary grades and beyond. Teaching these words occupies a special place in content areas such as science and social studies because words often have different and important meanings that are critical to comprehension in particular content areas. The meaning of *product* in mathematics and that of *legend* in geography are just two examples of such words.

Clarifying and Enriching the Meanings of Known Words. The meanings students originally attach to words are often imprecise and only become fully specified over time; thus another word-learning task is that of clarifying and enriching the meanings of already known words. For example, students initially might not recognize any difference between *brief* and *concise*, not know what distinguishes a *cabin* from a *shed*, or not realize that the term *virtuoso* is usually applied to those who play musical instruments. Although students will expand and enrich the meanings of the words they know as they repeatedly meet them in new and slightly different contexts, some more direct approaches to the matter are warranted.

Moving Words Into Students' Expressive Vocabularies. Still another word-learning task is that of moving words from students' receptive vocabularies to their productive vocabularies, that is, moving words from students' listening and reading vocabularies to their speaking and writing vocabularies. Sixth graders, for example, might know the meaning of the word *ignite* when they hear it or read it, yet never use the word themselves; and twelfth graders might know the word *huckster* but not use it. Most people actively use only a small percentage of the words they know. Assisting students in actively using the words they know will make them better and more precise communicators. This is particularly true of English learners, who are likely to have small expressive vocabularies as they begin learning English and who need a lot of practice and encouragement to use the words they know.

Building English Learners' Vocabularies. The last word-learning task I consider in this chapter is the unique situation faced by English learners. Ultimately, English learners need to learn the same words native speakers need to learn. But the task of doing so can be quite different in that they may have many more words to learn and may not have the same background knowledge that native speakers have. From a teacher's point of view, what is required is not so much different sorts of instruction, as understanding and appreciating the task English learners face and being able to adjust instruction accordingly.

Identifying and Selecting Vocabulary to Teach

Once you have considered the levels of word knowledge that you want your students to achieve and the word-learning tasks students face, you still have the task of selecting specific words to teach. Here, I recommend a two-step process in which you first get some idea of which words are likely to be unknown to your students and then follow several criteria for selecting the words.

Identifying Unknown Words. Three sources can be useful for identifying words to teach: word lists, the selections students are reading or listening to, and students themselves. One way in which word lists can be useful is in identifying a basic vocabulary of extremely frequent words that you want to be certain all students know. Although some notable efforts to create new lists of frequent words are currently underway (Biemiller, 2005; Hiebert, 2005), probably the best list to use at the present time is Fry's (2004) list of 1,000 Instant Words. This list is based on Carroll, Davies, and Richman's *American Heritage Word Frequency Book* (1971) described in Chapter 2, ranks the words according to their family frequencies, orders them from most frequent to least frequent, and is readily available. Note that using this list would not mean directly teaching 1,000 words because virtually all children will know some of them, and many children will know all of them. However, it is absolutely crucial that students master these words—initially in their oral vocabularies and then in their reading vocabularies—as soon as possible because they make up a huge percentage of the words they will come across as they read. The first 100 of them account for about 50% of the words students will encounter in what they read and the total 1,000 of them make up about 75% of the words they will encounter.

Another important list of frequent words, this one specifically for English learners, is the *General Service List of English Words* (West, 1953). Although the list was constructed some time ago and is based on British English, it continues to be useful and to be strongly recommended (Folse, 2004; Nation, 2001; Schmitt, 2000). One major advantage it has over the Fry list is that it gives the frequency of the various meanings of the words. Since many frequent words have multiple meanings, it is helpful to know which meanings are the most important ones to teach. Another advantage that the General Service List has over the Fry list is that it contains about twice as many words, approximately 2,000 word families. This is important because English learners need a basic vocabulary of about 2,000 words (Nation, 2001, Schmitt, 2000).

Another way in which word lists can be useful is in providing information about which words or sorts of words students are likely to know. Dale's list of 3,000 words (Chall & Dale, 1995) provides an alphabetical list of the 3,000 words that Dale's test data indicated were known by 80% or more of fourth graders. Studying this list will give you a feeling for the sorts of words that you do not need to teach most students in Grade 4 and above. A better but more difficult to obtain source for getting a feel for the words that students at various grade and ability levels are and are not likely to know is Dale and O'Rourke's *The Living Word Vocabulary* (1981). This book presents the results of vocabulary tests administered to students in Grades 4, 6, 8, 10, 12, 13, and 16. In all, the tests included about 43,000 items testing about 30,000 words, with several meanings of many of the words being tested. Each item on the test was administered to students at various grade levels until the grade level at which between 67% and 84% of the students tested correctly identified the meaning being tested. The text presents the word tested, the meaning tested, the grade level at which between 67% and 84% of the students knew the particular word-meaning combination, and the exact percentage of students at that grade level who correctly answered the item. The entry for *gratify*, which was tested with a single meaning, and the entry for *pose*, which was tested with four meanings, are shown in Figure 4.1. As can be seen, the test indicates that 67% of the eighth-grade students tested knew the word *gratify* with the meaning "to please." Each of the entries for *pose* provides similar information.

The Living Word Vocabulary thus provides precisely the information you need as you consider teaching a word. That is, it answers the question, "What percent of my students are likely to know this word with this meaning?" Moreover, research (Biemiller, 2004; Graves & Gebhart, 1982) has shown that the predictions are quite accurate. Of

Figure 4.1. Sample Entries from *The Living Word Vocabulary*

Grade	Score	Word	Meaning
8	67%	gratify	to please
4	80%	pose	to sit for an artist
6	80%	pose	to pretend
8	84%	pose	position
12	78%	pose	to present

course, looking up the meaning of each word you consider teaching is not feasible. However, the book is invaluable for getting a feel for what sorts of words students are likely to know at different grade levels. By identifying some words, predicting the percentages of students at a grade level who are likely to know them, and then checking your perceptions against the data in *The Living Word Vocabulary*, you can begin to develop a real feeling for the sorts of words that students at various ages do and do not know. Unfortunately, *The Living Word Vocabulary* is currently only available from libraries, but I believe it is informative enough to be worth searching out.

The second source useful for identifying words to teach—and the one that you will use the vast majority of the time—is the selections students are reading or listening to. As noted in Chapter 2, the English language consists of a small number of frequent words and a very large number of infrequent words. Once students acquire a basic vocabulary of several thousand words, the number of different words you might teach is so large that using word lists to identify words to teach becomes problematic. At this point, using your best judgment to select vocabulary from the material students are reading and listening to becomes the most reasonable approach to take. I discuss criteria for selecting vocabulary from texts students are reading in the next section of the chapter.

The third source of information about what words students do and do not know is the students themselves. As a way of sharpening your perceptions of which words your students are and are not likely to know, you can identify words in upcoming selections that you think will be difficult, build multiple-choice or matching tests on these words, and test students to find out whether or not the words are difficult. Of course, constructing such tests is time-consuming and certainly not something to be done for every selection. However, after several experiences of identifying words that you think will be difficult and then checking students' performance against your expectations, your general perceptions of which words are and are not likely to cause your students problems will become increasingly accurate.

In addition to testing students on potentially difficult words using multiple-choice or matching tests, you can take the opportunity to occasionally ask students which words they know. One easy way to do this is to list potentially difficult words on the board and have students raise their hands if they do not know a word. This approach is quick, easy, and risk free for students; it also gives students some responsibility for their word learning. Moreover, research (White, Slater, & Graves, 1989) indicates that students can be quite accurate in identifying words that they do and do not know.

Selecting Reading Vocabulary to Teach. As I just noted, once students have acquired a basic vocabulary, most of the words you teach should be selected for the material they are reading. Unfortunately, many reading selections will contain more difficult vocabulary than there is time to teach. Thus, once you have identified the potentially difficult vocabulary in a selection students are going to read, there is still the matter of deciding just which ones you will teach. The answers to the four questions listed below should be helpful in making that decision.

- *Is understanding the word important to understanding the selection in which it appears?* If the answer is yes, the word is a good candidate for instruction. If the answer is no, then other words are probably more important to teach.
- *Are students able to use context or structural-analysis skills to discover the word's meaning?* If they can use these skills, then they should be allowed to practice them. Doing so will both help them hone these skills and reduce the number of words to teach.
- *Can working with this word be useful in furthering students' context, structural-analysis, or dictionary skills?* If the answer here is yes, then working with the word can serve two purposes: It can aid students in learning the word and it can help them acquire a strategy they can use in learning other words. Teachers might, for example, decide to teach the word *regenerate* because students need to master the prefix *re-*.
- *How useful is this word outside of the reading selection currently being taught?* The more frequently a word appears in material students read, the more important it is for them to know the word. Additionally, the more frequent a word is, the greater the chances that students will retain the word once it is taught.

As a comment on these four questions, I need to add that they are not independent. In fact, the answer to one question may suggest that a word should be taught, while the answer to another may suggest that it should not, and authorities differ on which criterion should receive precedence. Beck and her colleagues (2002), for example, have suggested that precedence should be given to what they call Tier 2 words. As noted in Chapter 3, Tier 2 words are relatively high frequency words that are used by mature language users, that students are likely to encounter in the texts they read in upcoming years, and that are used across domains—for example, in English, and history, and science—and not just in a single domain such as health or music. Tier 2 words are certainly important, but in my judgment, teaching the words that are most important for understanding a particular selection will usually be the fore-most consideration. Ultimately, you will need to use your best judgment about which words to teach based on the demands of the reading selection and the needs of your students.

In concluding this section on selecting vocabulary to teach, I want to make a special comment about spelling. Teaching spelling needs to be clearly distinguished from teaching vocabulary. The vocabulary words that need to be taught are those that students don't know or cannot read. Spelling can be taught as a part of vocabulary instruction in order to reinforce word recognition, something that Juel and Deffes (2004) do in the Anchored Instruction approach described in Chapter 2. However, for the most part, the spelling words that students most need to be taught are words that they already know and are likely to need in their writing, but cannot spell. The procedures for teaching spelling are very different from those for teaching vocabulary. Although spelling is an important skill, it is not something I deal with in this book.

Some Guidelines for Vocabulary Instruction

One additional preliminary task remains: providing some general guidelines for vocabulary instruction. The following set of guidelines come from my own thinking and that of many other vocabulary authorities, including Herman and Dole (1988); Stahl (1998), Beck and her colleagues (2002), Biemiller (2004), and Nagy (2005). They are not absolutes and should be followed only when deemed appropriate. Moreover, they virtually always come at the cost of time, a factor I will consider after listing them.

- *Include both definitional and contextual information.* That is, give students both a definition of the words being taught, and have them work with the words in context.
- *Involve students in active and deep processing of the words.* Engage students in activities that lead them to consider the words' meaning, relate that meaning to information stored in memory, and work with the word in creative ways. Such activities might include putting the definition of a new word into their own words, giving examples and nonexamples of situations in which the word can be used, examining ways in which the new word relates to them personally, and recognizing similarities and differences between the new word and words they already know.
- *Provide students with multiple exposures to the word.* For example, define the word, use it in a sentence, ask students to use

it in a sentence, involve students in recognizing appropriate and not-so-appropriate uses of the word, and play games involving the word.

- *Review, rehearse, and remind students about the word in various contexts over time.* Teach a word before students read a selection and ask them to note its occurrence when reading the text. After students read, discuss the word and the context in which it occurred. Then, throughout the weeks and months following initial instruction, look for and point out other occurrences of the word, ask students to look for and point out other occurrences, and occasionally have a brief review of some of the words taught.
- *Involve students in discussions of the word's meaning.* Discussion is one method of actively processing word meanings, giving students the opportunity to hear and use the word in a variety of contexts and enabling students to learn from each other.
- *Spend a significant amount of time on the word.* During this time, involve students in actively grappling with the word's meaning. With words as with learning in general, time on task is crucial. The more time spent on a word, the better the chance that students will build rich and deep meanings for the word.

These are sound guidelines, but each of them should be prefaced with the phrase "for the strongest possible results." There is a definite cost of teaching in order to achieve the strongest possible results. Doing so takes time. Because there are many more words than can possibly be taught and because you have many things to do other than teach words, teachers' time is definitely limited. Often, it will be necessary to teach words in ways that do not consume large amounts of time and do not produce the strongest possible results. In these cases, think of your initial instruction on a word as just that—initial instruction, an initial experience that starts students on the long road to learning a full and rich meaning for the word.

METHODS OF TEACHING INDIVIDUAL WORDS

In this, the longest section of the chapter, I provide detailed descriptions of methods of teaching individual words that accomplish each of the word-learning tasks I have described. Note that the instruction needed for some word-learning tasks is much more complex than the instruction for others. Note, too, that instruction appropriate for some of these tasks will promote deeper levels of word knowledge than others.

Building Children's Oral Vocabularies

Building children's oral vocabularies was the major topic of Chapter 3 and will not be dealt with in this chapter. However, I do want to once again stress that for children who enter school with small vocabularies—linguistically disadvantaged children and some English learners—building their oral vocabularies is of utmost importance. As explained in Chapter 3, the primary vehicle for doing so is interactive oral reading.

Teaching Students to Read Known Words

In learning to read known words, the basic task for the student is to associate what is unknown, the written word, with what is already known, the spoken word. This is a decoding task. Students need to associate the written word, which they do not recognize, with the spoken word, which they know. To establish the association between the written and spoken forms of a word, students need to see the word at the same time that it is pronounced; and once the association is established, it needs to be rehearsed and strengthened so that the relationship becomes automatic. I have listed these steps below to emphasize just how straightforward the process is.

Procedure for Learning to Read Known Words

- See the word.
- Hear the word as it is seen.
- Rehearse that association a myriad of times.

Of course, there are a number of ways in which each of these steps can be accomplished. Students can see the word on the board, on a computer screen, or in a book that they are reading or you are reading to them. They can hear the word when you say it, when another student says it, or when a voice simulator on a computer says it. They can rehearse the association by seeing the word and pronouncing it a number of times, writing it, and playing games that require them to recognize printed versions of it. However, wide reading in materials that contain many repetitions of the words and that are enjoyable and easily read by students is by far the best form of rehearsal for these words and an essential part of students' mastering them.

While the simple three-step procedure for teaching students to read known words will get the job done, you may want to use a more powerful procedure. Anchored Instruction (Juel & Deffes, 2003), which was described in detail in Chapter 3, is a more powerful alternative. As you will recall, Anchored Instruction deals with the word's meaning, some aspects of decoding, and spelling. Dealing with meaning makes good sense if you are not certain that all of your students have the words in their oral vocabularies, and dealing with decoding and spelling will of course reinforce students' skills in these important areas. At the same time, this more powerful instruction will require more of your time and more of your students' time.

Teaching New Words Representing Known Concepts

Here, I describe three approaches to teaching new words representing known concepts. These require differing amounts of teacher time, differing amounts of class time, and differing amounts of students' time and effort; and they are likely to yield different results.

The first method, Context-Dictionary-Discussion, takes the least amount of preparation on your part while taking a fair amount of students' time. It will provide students with a basic understanding of a word's meaning and give them practice in using the dictionary. As shown below, it consists of three steps. In this and most of the descriptions of teaching methods I give, I will present examples of the instruction using two words, one typical of words for primary or elementary students and one typical of words for middle school and secondary students.

Context-Dictionary-Discussion Procedure

- Give students the word in context.
- Ask them to look it up in the dictionary.
- Discuss the definitions they come up with.

excel
To get into the Olympics, a person must really *excel at* some Olympic sport.

subscript
Nicole, a student in Ms. Green's third hour mathematics class, had used the term x to refer to three different quantities, and thus she added *subscripts* to distinguish the three terms.

The second method, Definition Plus Rich Context, takes a fair amount of preparation time on your part, but it takes very little class time. It too will provide students with a basic understanding of a word's meaning and consists of three steps.

Definition-Plus-Rich-Context Procedure

- Give students a definition for the word.
- Give them the word in a rich context.
- Discuss the definition, the context, and some other contexts in which the word might be used.

vital—extremely important, perhaps even necessary
In areas in which water is very scarce, it is *vital* that everyone takes extra precautions to ensure that no water is wasted.

irradiate—to treat something or someone with radiation
It's becoming increasingly common to *irradiate* meat and some other foods to kill potentially harmful bacteria.

The third method, the Context-Relationship Procedure (Graves & Slater, in press), takes quite a bit of preparation time on your part. However, presenting words in this way takes only about a minute per word, and we have repeatedly found that students remember quite rich meanings for words taught in this fashion. Here is how it is done.

Context-Relationship Procedure

- Create a brief paragraph that uses the target word three or four times and in doing so gives the meaning of the word.
- Follow the paragraph with a multiple-choice item that checks students' understanding of the word.
- Show the paragraph (probably on an overhead), read it aloud, and read the multiple-choice options.
- Pause to give students a moment to answer the multiple-choice item, give them the correct answer, and discuss the word and any questions they have.

Conveying
The luncheon speaker was successful in *conveying* his main ideas to the audience. They all understood what he said, and most agreed with him. *Conveying* has a more specific meaning

than *talking*. *Conveying* indicates that a person is getting his or
her ideas across accurately.
Conveying means
        _____ A.   putting parts together.
        _____ B.   communicating a message.
        _____ C.   hiding important information.

Rationale
The *rationale* for my wanting to expose students to a variety of
words and their meanings is partially that this will help them
become better thinkers who are able to express their ideas more
clearly. Part of that *rationale* also includes my belief that words
themselves are fascinating objects of study. My *rationale* for
doing something means my fundamental reasons for doing it.
Rationale means
        _____ A.   a deliberate error.
        _____ B.   the basis for doing something.
        _____ C.   a main idea for an essay.

The fourth method, Rich Instruction, is designed to give students deep
and lasting understanding of word meanings. It can also be used to teach
new concepts if the concepts are not too difficult and students have some
information related to them. The procedure has been described in several publications by Beck and McKeown and their colleagues (Beck et al.,
1982; Beck et al., 2002; McKeown & Beck, 2004) and has taken several
forms. Here is a version that can be used in a number of situations. For
the sake of simplicity, this example deals with a single word—*ambitious*.
Often, however, Rich Instruction is used to teach a set of words.

Rich Instruction

- Begin with a student-friendly definition.
    ambitious—really wanting to succeed at something
- Arrange for students to work with the word more than once. One
    encounter with a word is very unlikely to leave students with a
    rich and lasting understanding of its meaning. Two is a minimum,
    but more are desirable.
- Provide the word in more than one context so that students' under-
    standing is not limited to one situation. The several contexts need
    not come at the same time.
    Susan's *ambition* to become an Olympic high jumper was so
    strong that she was willing to practice 6 hours a day.

Rupert had never been an *ambitious* person, and after his accident he did little other than watch television.

- Engage students in activities in which they need to deal with various facets of the word's meaning and with investigating relationships between the target word and other words.

    Would you like to have a really *ambitious* person as a friend? Why or why not?

    Which of the following better demonstrates *ambition*? (1) A stockbroker gets up every day and goes to work. (2) A stockbroker stays late at work every day, trying to close as many deals as possible before leaving.

    How likely is it that an *ambitious* person would be *lethargic*? How likely is it that an *ambitious* person would be *energetic*? Explain your answers.

- Have students create uses for the words.

    Tell me about a friend that you see as very *ambitious*. What are some of the things he does that show how *ambitious* he is?

- Encourage students to use the word outside of class.

    Come to class tomorrow prepared to talk about someone who appears to be ambitious. This could be a stranger you happen to notice outside of class, someone in your family, someone you read about, or someone you see on TV.

Quite obviously, Rich Instruction will create deep and lasting understanding of words. Equally obviously, Rich Instruction takes a great deal of time, certainly more time than you can spend on most words you teach. You will need to decide just when to use it.

Teaching New Words Representing New Concepts

The dividing line between words that represent known concepts and those that represent new concepts is not a precise one. Words fall on a continuum, ranging from those that clearly represent known concepts to those that clearly represent new and challenging concepts. Moreover, a word that is likely to be a new concept for most fourth graders may be a familiar concept for most tenth graders. For example, the word *ecological* might represent a new concept for most fourth graders but a familiar one for most tenth graders, while the word *margin* (as in buying stocks on margin) is likely to represent a new concept to anyone not familiar with the stock market. This section describes two very powerful procedures for teaching new and potentially challenging concepts, while the upcoming section on Clarifying and Enriching the

Meanings of Known Words describes several other procedures that can be used to teach new concepts. The first procedure described here was developed by Frayer, Frederick, and Klausmeier (1969) and is often called the Frayer Method. It is an extremely powerful although definitely time-consuming approach. Here I present the major steps of the methods with examples for the word/concept *globe* and the word/concept *perseverance*.

Frayer Method

1. Define the new concept, giving its necessary attributes. When feasible, it is also helpful to show a picture illustrating the concept.

    A *globe* is a spherical (ball-like) representation of a planet. *Perseverance* is a trait that a person might possess. A person demonstrates *perseverance* when he remains constant to some purpose or task over some extended period despite obstacles.

2. Distinguish between the new concept and similar but different concepts with which it might be mistaken. In doing so, it may be appropriate to identify some accidental attributes that might falsely be considered to be necessary attributes of the new concept.

    A *globe* is different from a *map* because a map is flat. A *globe* is different from a *contour map*, a map in which mountains and other high points are raised above the general level of the map, because a contour map is not spherical.

    Perseverance differs from *stubbornness* in that *perseverance* is typically seen as a positive quality and the goal toward which one perseveres is typically a worthwhile one. Conversely, *stubbornness* is usually seen as a negative quality, and the goal pursued by a person who is being stubborn is often not a worthwhile one.

3. Give examples of the concept and explain why they are examples.

    The most common *globe* is a globe of the earth. *Globes* of the earth are spherical and come in various sizes and colors. A much less common *globe* is a globe of another planet. A museum might have a spherical representation of Saturn.

    A person who graduates from college despite financial responsibilities that require him to work full-time while in college would be demonstrating *perseverance* because the goal is worthwhile and it takes a long and steady effort to reach it.

A person who learns to ski after losing a leg in an accident is demonstrating *perseverance* for similar reasons.
4. Give nonexamples of the concept.

A map of California is not a *globe* because it is flat.

A map of how to get to a friend's house is not a *globe* because it is not spherical.

Someone who goes fishing a lot just because he enjoys it is not demonstrating *perseverance* because there is no particular purpose here and no obstacles.

Someone who waters his lawn once a week is not demonstrating *perseverance* because there is no particular challenge in doing so.
5. Present students with examples and nonexamples and ask them to distinguish between the two.

For *globe*:

An aerial photograph of New York (nonexample)

A red sphere representing Mars (example)

A walking map of St. Louis (nonexample)

A ball-shaped model of the moon (example)

For *perseverance*:

Reading an interesting book that you thoroughly enjoy (nonexample)

Completing a canoe trip from the headwaters of the Mississippi to New Orleans (example)

Eating a dozen donuts because you are really hungry (nonexample)

Completing a 3-mile cross-country race even though you were out of breath and dead tired after less than a mile (example)
6. Have students present examples and nonexamples of the concept, have them explain why they are examples or nonexamples, and give them feedback on their examples and explanations.

The second procedure I suggest for teaching new and challenging concepts was described by Nagy (1988), who took it from an unpublished paper by Little. It requires less teacher time, although it still requires a good deal of class time. I call it Focused Discussion. In the following discussion, the key concept is *stereotype*.

Focused Discussion

Divide the class into two groups, assigning a recorder for each group. The groups will each be brainstorming word associations. One group should be brainstorming as many words or phrases as they can connected with the word *city*. The other group should brainstorm words or phrases connected with the phrase *small towns*. The recorder in each group should write down the words and phrases brainstormed.

After giving the groups about 3 minutes for the brainstorming session, ask each recorder to read the group's list. Encourage students to ask questions about the words and allow them to express further ideas about the aptness of the words on their lists. Then introduce the concept of stereotype to the students, explaining it in terms of oversimplified and formulaic views and attitudes about people, places, and institutions. Ask the students whether or not any of the ideas on their lists reflect stereotypes of big cities or small towns and the people who live in them. Spend some time discussing stereotypes, noting that people and places do not often fit the stereotyped images used to describe them. (Nagy, 1988, p. 22)

Teaching concepts with either the Frayer Method or Focused Discussion takes a good deal of time. The methods also require a good deal of thought on the part of both you and your students. However, the fruits of the labor are well worth the effort, for with these methods students can gain a new idea, another lens through which they can interpret the world. Moreover, if students need to learn a difficult concept, teaching it is going to take some time. Teaching a new and difficult concept as though it is merely a new label—for example, teaching it using the Context-Dictionary-Discussion Procedure—will not get the job done.

Teaching New Meanings for Known Words

New meanings for known words may or may not represent new concepts for students. If the new meanings do not represent new and difficult concepts, the procedure for teaching new meanings for known words is fairly simple and straightforward. The approach termed Introducing New Meanings is one appropriate method.

Introducing New Meanings

1. Acknowledge the known meaning.
2. Give the new meaning.
3. Note the similarities between the meanings (if any).

Product
1. something made by a company
2. the number made by multiplying other numbers

3. The similarity is that in both instances something is produced or made by some process.

Wax
1. a material used to make candles and polish things
2. to grow bigger
3. In this case, there does not appear to be any similarity in the meanings.

If the new meanings to be learned represent new and difficult concepts, then Frayer's approach to teaching concepts described earlier or the methods described in the next section are more appropriate.

Clarifying and Enriching the Meanings of Known Words

Here, I present four methods of clarifying and enriching the meanings of known words. These methods are also useful in preteaching unknown words to improve comprehension of a selection that includes them. And they can be used to teach new concepts, if the concepts are not too difficult and students have at least some information related to them.

Possible Sentences

Possible Sentences is a procedure that Stahl and Kapinus (1991) have shown to be useful for teaching words from informational texts. With this procedure, the teacher begins by choosing six to eight words that might cause difficulty for students from an upcoming selection. These should represent key concepts and related words. Next, the teacher selects an additional four to six words that are likely to be familiar to students. These familiar words are used to help students generate sentences.

Once the 10 to 12 words are selected, they are put on the board. If some students in the class know the definitions, they can define them. If not, you should provide short definitions. Following this, students are told to create sentences that use at least two of the words and that are *possible sentences* in the selection they are about to read; that is, students create sentences that could appear in the upcoming selection. The sentences students create are then put on the board and students are instructed to read the selection.

Following the reading of the selection, you return to the sentences on the board and the class discusses whether each of them could or could not be true given the content of the reading selection. Sentences that could be true are left as they are. Sentences that could not be true are discussed by the class and modified so that they could be true.

Shown here are some of the words Stahl and Kapinus selected from some science texts they worked with and a few of the possible sentences students might generate with the words:

- Potentially difficult words: *front, barometer, humidity, air mass, air pressure,* and *meteorology*
- Familiar words: *clouds, rain,* and *predict*
- When a *front* approaches it is quite likely to *rain.* (could be true)
- Most people don't like days with a lot of *humidity* or with a lot of *clouds.* (could be true)
- When a *front* approaches, it is very unlikely to *rain.* (could not be true)

Semantic Mapping

The second method of clarifying and extending the meanings of known words, and of introducing vocabulary in a way that is likely to improve comprehension of a selection, is Semantic Mapping (Heimlich & Pittelman, 1986). With this method, the teacher puts a word representing a central concept on the chalkboard; asks students to work in groups listing as many words related to the central concept as they can; writes students' words on the chalkboard grouped in broad categories; has students name the categories and perhaps suggest additional ones; and discusses with students the central concept, the other words, the categories, and their interrelationships. Figure 4.2 shows a semantic map for the word *tenement* that students might create before or after reading a social studies chapter on urban housing.

Figure 4.3 shows a semantic map for the word *telecommunications.* Since many students know a good deal about telecommunications, it might work well for them to begin the map before reading a selection dealing with the topic and then complete the map after they have read the passage.

Semantic Feature Analysis

Semantic Feature Analysis (Pittelman et al., 1991) is particularly suited to refining word meanings.

1. Present students with a grid that contains a set of related words on one axis and a list of features that each of the words may or

Figure 4.2. Semantic Map for the Word *Tenement*

Conditions	*Owners*
Run down	Hard to reach
Small	Make good money
Crowded	Don't live there
Drab	Often don't care

TENEMENT

Costs	*Tenants*
Not cheap	People without a lot of money
Lower than some places	New immigrants
Too high	City people
	Large families

may not have on the other axis. Figure 4.4 shows a grid for *roads and walkways*.

2. In their first work with semantic feature analysis, show students a completed grid and discuss how the plus and minus signs indicate whether or not a particular feature applies to each word.
3. In later work with the procedure, show students grids with the terms and attributes filled in but without the pluses and minuses and ask students to insert them.
4. Later still, show grids with some terms and some attributes and ask students to add to both the list of related words and the list of attributes, and then to fill in the plus and minus signs.
5. Finally, after students are proficient in working with partially completed grids you supply, they can create their own grids for sets of related words they suggest.

As with many techniques for vocabulary instruction, as part of semantic feature analysis there should be a good deal of discussion, for much of the power of the procedure lies in the discussion. With the roads and walkways grid, for example, discussion of the fact that *boulevards, freeways,* and *turnpikes* share the same features should lead to a discussion of whether additional attributes should be added in order to distinguish among these. Alternately, you and your students might conclude that these three terms are synonyms.

Another semantic feature analysis grid, this one for the term *vehicles* is shown in Figure 4.5.

Figure 4.3. Semantic Map for the Word *Telecommunications*

Costs
nothing
$100s
$1,000s
$1,000,000s

Users	*Types of*
government	radio Direct TV
businesses	television cable
education	phone lines the web
individuals	the Internet

TELECOMMUNICATIONS

Places Where It Is Used	*Potential Problems*
homes	costs
schools	standardization
offices	compatibility
cars	training

Potential Benefits
instant communications
easy access to information
opportunities for collaborating
saving time and money
recreation
entertainment

Venn Diagrams

Venn Diagrams represent a fourth possibility for clarifying and extending word meanings. With Venn diagrams, you typically investigate the meanings of two similar words, in the process figuring out which attributes the words share, which are exclusive to one word, and which are exclusive to the other word.

- Choose two words with similar but not precisely the same meanings.
- Draw an empty Venn Diagram, two overlapping circles, on the chalkboard or an overhead.

Figure 4.4. Semantic Feature Analysis Grid for *Roads and Walkways*

Roads and Walkways	Typical Characteristics					
	narrow	wide	paved	unpaved	for walking	for driving
path	+	−	−	+	+	−
trail	+	−	−	+	+	−
road	+	+	+	+	−	+
lane	+	−	+	+	+	+
boulevard	−	+	+	−	−	+
freeway	−	+	+	−	−	+
turnpike	−	+	+	−	−	+

- Discuss the meaning common to both words and the meaning unique to each word and fill in the Venn Diagram accordingly.
- Alternately, students can complete Venn Diagrams in pairs or small groups and share their findings with the class.

Figure 4.6 shows a Venn Diagram for the terms *short stories* and *essays*.

Figure 4.5. Semantic Feature Analysis Grid for *Vehicle*

Vehicle	Typical Characteristics					
	two wheels	four wheels	more than four wheels	motor	diesel fuel	gasoline fuel
car	−	+	−	+	−	+
bicycle	+	−	−	−	−	−
motorcycle	+	−	−	+	−	+
truck	−	−	+	+	+	−
train	−	−	+	+	+	−
skateboard	−	+	−	−	−	−
sailboat	−	−	−	−	−	−
iceboat	−	−	−	−	−	−

Figure 4.6. Venn Diagram for the Terms *Short Stories* and *Essays*

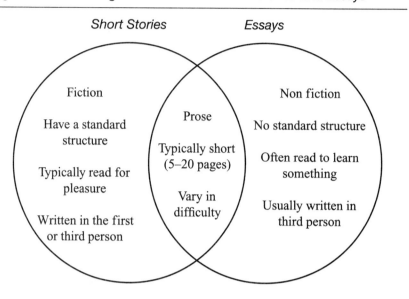

Short Stories   Essays

Fiction

Have a standard
structure

Typically read for
pleasure

Written in the first
or third person

Prose

Typically short
(5–20 pages)

Vary in
difficulty

Non fiction

No standard structure

Often read to learn
something

Usually written in
third person

Moving Words Into Students' Expressive Vocabularies

Students can be encouraged to move words into their expressive vocabularies by your providing a model of precise word use, your encouraging students to employ precise and mature words in their speech and writing and recognizing appropriate diction when they display it, and your providing time and encouragement for various sorts of word play that prompt students to work with words they might otherwise not speak or write. Probably the best opportunity to help students build their expressive vocabularies is when they are honing their writing or finalizing relatively formal oral presentations. One of the last steps that professional writers and public speakers take in finalizing their work is to examine their word choices. Doing so might involve asking themselves several questions about the words they have used.

Some Questions About Word Choices

- Do the words I have used precisely convey my meaning?
- Are they at an appropriate level of sophistication for my audience?
- Are they appropriately forceful and colorful for my topic?

In addition to routinely emphasizing the importance of the words students use in their speech and writing, it makes good sense to occasionally put the spotlight on words in some concentrated and robust instruction. Duin (Duin & Graves, 1987, 1988) developed and tested an approach to such concentrated and robust instruction modeled on the Rich Instruction that Beck and McKeown developed. Duin's approach, Expressive Vocabulary Instruction, can be used with upper elementary through junior high students to focus their attention on the words they use in their writing over a period of a week or so.

Expressive Vocabulary Instruction

- Words are taught in groups of 10 or so related words presented over a 3- to 6-day period. The words are not necessarily semantically related, but they do lend themselves to writing on a particular topic. A set of words Duin has used with an essay about *space* includes *feasible, accommodate, tether, criteria, module, retrieve, configuration,* and *quest.*
- Students work extensively with the words, spending about half an hour a day with the 10 to 15 words taught during the 3 to 6 days of instruction and doing five to ten activities with each word.
- Instruction is deliberately varied in order to accomplish various purposes. Students define words, use them in sentences, do speeded trials with them, make affective responses to them, compare them to each other and to other concepts, keep a written record of their work with them, use them outside of class, and do several short writing assignments with them.
- Examples of the tasks Duin has used include the following: Students discussed how *feasible* space travel might soon be for each of them. They were asked if they thought their school could find a way to better *accommodate* handicapped students. They distinguished between new words, such as *retrieve,* and related words, such as *return,* by filling in sentence frames with the more appropriate of the two words. They wrote brief essays called "Space Shorts," employing the words in dealing with such topics as the foods that would be available in space, and judged each other's use of the words.

Duin's work has indicated that students working with this sort of instruction use a substantial proportion of the taught words in essays targeted to using the words and that the essays of students who have received the instruction are judged markedly superior to those of students who have not received it. Equally important, her work has shown that students thoroughly enjoy learning and using words in this way. These findings can be taken as a recommendation for helping and encouraging students to experiment with new, precise, and vivid vocabulary in their writing.

Building English Learners' Vocabularies

As reviews by Fitzgerald (1995), Gersten and Baker (2000), and Slavin and Cheung (2003) clearly indicate, instructional approaches that are effective with native English speakers are likely to be effective with English learners. Moreover, Schmitt (2000), the RAND Reading Study Group (2002), and Carlo and her colleagues (2004) have seen promise for English learners in the four-part program I describe in this book. Thus this section does not describe different methods for teaching English learners. Instead, it notes several of the particular challenges that English learners face, and discusses some general approaches to helping them meet these challenges.

There are a number of challenges that English learners face in developing their vocabularies. Here I concentrate on four of them. The first is building a basic vocabulary of the most frequent English words. Like the primary-grade children described in Chapter 3, some English learners have very small English vocabularies. With such students, the most pressing need is that they build a basic oral and reading vocabulary consisting of the 2,000 or so most frequent English words (Nation, 2001; Schmitt, 2000). As noted earlier in the chapter, the *General Service List* (West, 1953), which shows the frequency of the various meanings of the 2,000 most frequent words, is widely recommended. Because these words appear so frequently, we need to ensure that students know them. For primary-grade English learners, the sorts of interactive oral reading described in Chapter 3 are appropriate approaches. For older students, some combination of directly teaching the words, encouraging students to systematically study and learn them on their own, and having students do a lot of reading in simple material made up almost exclusively of these words is an appropriate approach. Second-language specialists such as Nation (2001) and Schmitt (2000) offer a number of additional approaches. Ideally, a special language teacher should plan the approach to be used and be primarily responsible for this instruction, but if no special language teacher is available, classroom teachers need to do what they can.

A second challenge English learners face is that of building a vocabulary of academic English. As Cummins (2003) has explained, while

1 or 2 years may be sufficient for English learners to master conversational English, research indicates that "at least 5 years (and frequently more) are required for students to bridge the gap in academic English between them and their native English-speaking peers" (p. 4). In bridging this gap, English learners face a task that is in many ways the same that native speakers face—learning large numbers of relatively infrequent words. As is also the case with native speakers, the major source of academic English is the texts students are reading. The difference, however, is that native speakers already know many more of these words. Thus a text that might include 5 unknown words for native speakers, might include 10 or more unknown words for some English learners. Be aware of this possibility as you select vocabulary to teach. You will almost certainly need to teach more academic words to English learners than to native English speakers. An additional source of academic words for high school English learners who plan to go on to college is the Academic Word List (Coxhead, 2000), a list of 570 word families that occur in many academic texts.

A third challenge English learners face is the thousands of idioms in the language. Terms like "kill the goose that laid the golden egg" and "put your money where your mouth is" are not the literal meanings of the individual words that make them up and must be learned as unique units.

A fourth challenge is that English words that merely represent new labels for native speakers may represent new concepts for English learners. This is a challenge for you as well as your students, because there is no very direct way for you to know just which words do and do not represent new concepts. The approach I recommend is to recognize this possibility, realize that the greater the difference between English learners' backgrounds and cultures and those of native speakers the more likely it is that there will be many concepts that come up in class that are unfamiliar to them, and be prepared to use appropriate procedures for teaching new concepts when the need arises.

I turn now to some general approaches to dealing with these challenges. First, take advantage of cognates, particularly with Spanish-speaking students. Depending on what sorts of words and what sorts of texts are considered, it has been estimated that from 20% to over 30% of English words have Spanish cognates (Kamil & Bernhardt, 2004; Kamil & Hiebert, 2005). In teaching words that have cognates, note that fact and identify the cognates for students. Second, make use of glossaries. When upcoming selections contain more unknown words than you can teach, create and hand out glossaries of them. While glossaries are certainly not as effective as powerful teaching methods, they can be a substantial aid to English learners. Third, become aware of idioms and point them out to students when they occur. In doing so, sources like the *Longman American Idioms Dictionary* (1999), which lists over 4,000 idioms, will prove useful. Fourth, modify the specific procedures described in this chapter to make them more powerful and more appropriate for English learners. For example, if a word has a cognate, add a step in which you identify and highlight that cognate to approaches like the Context-Dictionary-Discussion Procedure. Similarly, if a word seems particularly difficult, add some Rich Instruction activities to approaches like the Context-Relationship Procedure. For example, after students answer the multiple-choice item—the last step in the Context-Relationship Procedure—you might have them identify a situation to which the word being taught could apply. With the word *rationale,* you might ask students to "Describe a situation in which you would probably need to give the principal a *rationale* for your actions." The final general approach to helping English learners deal with the challenges of learning vocabulary is to teach them word-learning strategies, the topic of the next chapter. While word-learning strategies are important for all students, they are particularly important for English learners because of the very large number of words they need to learn.

SELECTING AMONG THE METHODS AND TEACHING VOCABULARY TO IMPROVE READING COMPREHENSION

In the preceding section, I discussed eight different word-learning tasks and over a dozen instructional procedures. Although this is a lot of procedures and there is wide agreement that different procedures are needed for different tasks (Kamil & Hiebert, 2005; National Reading Panel, 2000; RAND Reading Study Group, 2002), I do not want to suggest that choosing a procedure should be difficult and time-consuming. Nor is it the case that only one procedure is appropriate in any one situation. For example, the procedures suggested for "Clarifying and Enriching the Meanings of Known Words" can also be used for "Teaching New Words Representing Known Concepts" (this would be particularly robust instruction for the task) or for "Teaching New Words Representing New Concepts" (this would not be as robust as the procedures listed there). Additionally, you may want to choose half a dozen or so of the procedures and use them repeatedly, so that both you and your students are familiar with them. Moreover, when you are preteaching vocabulary before students read a section—something that you are likely to do frequently—you are likely to use only one or two procedures, even though the words represent somewhat different learning tasks. Using more than one or two procedures at a time is likely to become cumbersome and is not necessary.

The topic of preteaching vocabulary leads naturally to the topic of teaching vocabulary to improve comprehension, a frequent and very important goal of vocabulary instruction. The richer the instruction is, the more thoughtful processing it requires of students; and the more it is focused on important content of the selection that students are reading or are about to read, the greater the likelihood that the instruction you provide will improve students' comprehension of the selection they are reading or are about to read. Thus, procedures like Rich Instruction, the Frayer Method, Focused Discussion, Possible Sentences, Semantic Mapping, Semantic Feature Analysis, and Venn Diagrams are particularly likely to improve comprehension. At the same time, all of these procedures take valuable classroom time, and you will need to decide when to use these more powerful procedures and when some less powerful ones will be more appropriate.

CONCLUDING REMARKS

Although teaching individual words is only one part of a comprehensive vocabulary program, it is a very important part. It is also a relatively complex part in terms of both planning and delivering the instruction. Planning involves recognizing the part that teaching individual words plays in students' overall vocabulary development, considering the levels of word knowledge you want students to achieve, and selecting vocabulary to teach. Instruction involves identifying the word-learning task or tasks represented by the words you are teaching, choosing an appropriate method of instruction, and of course creating and providing that instruction. My goal in this chapter has been to provide you with the information you need to do all of this and do it well.

To that end, I have concentrated on appropriate approaches for teaching individual words and have described over a dozen of them. There are, however, a number of inappropriate approaches. In concluding the chapter, I briefly list several things NOT to do when teaching vocabulary.

Things NOT to Do in Teaching Vocabulary

- Don't give students words out of context and ask them to look them up in the dictionary.

- Don't have students do speeded trials with individual words.
- Don't have students complete word mazes.
- Don't teach words as though they are new labels for existing concepts when they represent new and challenging concepts.
- Don't teach spelling when you mean to be teaching vocabulary. Teaching spelling is certainly important, but teaching both spelling and vocabulary will require more time than teaching only vocabulary. You need to decide when you want to spend that additional time.
- Don't assume that context will typically yield precise word meanings.

One other thing we should not assume is that students can use context, word parts, or the dictionary to learn words without having been taught how to do so. How to teach these powerful word-learning strategies is the topic of Chapter 5.

Teaching Word-Learning Strategies

For every word known by a child who is able to apply morphology and context, an additional one to three words should be understandable.
William Nagy and Richard Anderson, Vocabulary Researchers

Teaching students word-learning strategies—strategies such as using context and word parts to unlock the meanings of words they don't know—is tremendously important. With tens of thousands of words to learn, anything we can do to help students become more proficient independent word learners is an absolute necessity. Fortunately, we can do a lot to sharpen students' skills at learning words on their own. This, as Nagy and Anderson (1994) suggest, will enable students to more than double the number of words they learn.

In this chapter, I discuss five ways in which we can help students become increasingly competent at learning words on their own. These are

- Using Context to Unlock the Meanings of Unknown Words
- Using Word Parts to Unlock the Meanings of Unknown Words
- Using the Dictionary and Related Reference Tools
- Developing a Strategy for Dealing with Unknown Words
- Adopting a Personal Approach to Building Their Vocabularies

Before describing instruction to build students' competence in each of these important areas, I will first describe a very powerful general model for teaching strategies, a model that underlies all of the instructional procedures I discuss in this chapter.

A POWERFUL MODEL FOR TEACHING STRATEGIES

A substantial body of theory and research has supported two approaches to teaching strategies—direct explanation of strategies and transactional strategies instruction (Sales & Graves, 2005). *Direct explanation of strategies* has been repeatedly validated and endorsed over the past 2 decades (e.g., Duffy, 2002; Duffy et al., 1987; Duke & Pearson, 2002; Graves, Juel, & Graves, 2004; National Reading Panel, 2000; Pearson, Roehler, Dole, & Duffy; 1992, RAND Reading Study Group, 2002; Sweet & Snow, 2003). Direct explanation of strategies is a very explicit, step-by-step approach. Usually, carefully prepared materials specifically designed to facilitate students learning the strategy and carefully preplanned lessons are used. A typical unit that is used to initially teach a strategy might last from several days to several weeks. Such a unit begins with the teacher doing the bulk of the work—explaining the strategy, noting its importance, modeling its use, and the like. Then, gradually, the instruction is modified so that students assume primary responsibility for use of the strategy.

The basic components of direct explanation of strategies are listed below.

- An explicit description of the strategy and when and how it should be used
- Teacher and/or student modeling of the strategy in action
- Collaborative use of the strategy in action
- Guided practice using the strategy with gradual release of responsibility
- Independent use of the strategy (Duke & Pearson, 2002, pp. 208–210)

Following these steps is a powerful, effective, and efficient way to initially teach a strategy. Used by itself, however, direct explanation may be too artificial and too separated from the ongoing activities of the classroom. Students may learn to use the strategy during the special periods set aside for strategy instruction but then fail to use it when they are reading at other times of the school day and outside of school.

In response to this problem, Pressley and his colleagues developed *transactional strategies instruction*. It too has been validated in a number of studies (e.g., Brown, Pressley, Van Meter, & Schuder, 1996; Pressley, 2000, 2002; Pressley, El-Dinary, et al., 1992; Reutzel, Fawson, & Smith, 2003). Like direct explanation, transactional strategies instruction includes some direct explanation as part of the initial instruction. Compared to direct explanation, however, transactional strategies instruction is much less structured, and the period of direct explanation is likely to be brief. Moreover, transactional strategies instruction is introduced as part of the ongoing reading activities in the classroom when the occasion arises for students to use a particular strategy. This means that the instruction cannot be preplanned and special materials to facilitate teaching it cannot be prepared in advance. Although there is solid evidence that transactional instruction is effective, there is also clear evidence that relatively few teachers can and do learn to use transactional strategies instruction (Pressley & El-Dinary, 1997; Pressley, 2002). Because it is an on-the-fly approach and not supported by a specific curriculum and instructional materials, teachers have found it very difficult to work transactional strategies instruction into the school day.

The approach described in this chapter, *balanced strategies instruction*, combines these two approaches and modifies them in several ways. Balanced strategies instruction is initially more deliberate and carefully planned than transactional instruction but later on includes more review, rehearsal, integration, and constructivist activities than direct explanation. Additionally, balanced strategies instruction includes more direct attention to motivation and engagement than is often included in the other two types of strategies instruction. Finally, in keeping with the approach to strategy instruction described by Paris, Lipson, and Wixson (1983), with balanced strategies instruction, students are given declarative, procedural, and conditional knowledge. That is, they receive detailed knowledge about the strategies, they learn how to actually use them, and they learn when to use them.

Here are some guidelines to follow when working with balanced strategies instruction, guidelines modified from suggestions given by Pressley, Harris, and Marks (1992).

- In the initial planning of instruction, at the beginning of the actual instruction, throughout the initial instruction, and in follow-up activities, teachers give substantial attention to motivating students to use the strategies, particularly by highlighting the empowerment that comes when students use the strategies on important academic tasks.
- Teachers fully explain and discuss with students the value of the strategies and rationales for using them, including why strategies aid performance and when they can be used profitably.
- Teachers extensively model the strategies and provide verbal explanations and collaborative discussion of the thinking processes associated with strategy steps.
- Teachers provide extensive feedback and engage in substantial collaborative discussion with students as they try strategies.
- Instruction and practice extend over a long period of time and across diverse tasks.

- Teachers and students determine opportunities for transfer, not just during initial instruction but also during the weeks, months, and even years following the initial instruction.
- Teachers encourage habitual reflection and planning. Assisting students in appropriately using word-learning strategies is one part of the larger goal of making students metacognitive in their learning.

USING CONTEXT CLUES

Using context clues to infer the meanings of unknown words is the first word-learning strategy I consider because it is the most important one. Most words are learned from context, and if we can increase students' proficiency in learning from context even a small amount, we will greatly increase the number of words students learn. It is therefore vital to provide students with rich, sustained, and powerful instruction on using context clues. Providing such instruction takes a good deal of time and effort on the part of both teachers and students. The instruction outlined here takes place over ten 30–45-minute sessions. A sample schedule is shown in Figure 5.1. In what follows, I describe the first two days of instruction in some detail and then much more briefly describe the rest of the unit. The instruction is described as it would be presented to students in the upper elementary grades. With older students, the language and examples would be somewhat more sophisticated.

Day 1—Introduction and Motivation

Because learning to use context clues is a demanding and challenging task, the teacher introduces the unit with a substantial motivational activity designed to both gain students' interest and enable them to relate the task of using context clues to infer word meanings to an activity they are familiar with—using a VCR.

She begins by telling students that over the next few weeks the class is going to be working on using context clues to figure out the meanings of unknown words they come across while reading. Using clues to figure out things they don't know, she tells them, is something they do all the time, something they're good at, and something that is fun. Then, she tells them that they'll begin their study of context clues by viewing a brief video showing a place they might know and that their job is to look for clues to what the place is.

Figure 5.1. Overview of a Unit on Context Clues

DAY 1	DAY 2	DAY 3	DAY 4	DAY 5
Motivation and introduction to using context to infer meaning using a videotape	Introduction to using context clues to infer word meanings and to the four-step strategy	Detailed instruction in the first two steps of the strategy: Play and Question, and Slow Advance	Detailed instruction in the second two steps of the strategy: Stop and Rewind, and Play and Question	Game in which students earn points for using the four-step strategy to infer word meanings
DAY 6	**DAY 7**	**DAY 8**	**DAY 9**	**DAY 10**
Review of using context clues and the four-step strategy; renaming of the four steps without the VCR terminology	Guided practice—and further instruction if necessary—in using the four-step process with teacher-provided narrative texts.	Guided practice—and further instruction if necessary—in using the four-step process with teacher-provided expository texts.	Guided practice—and further instruction if necessary—in using the four-step process with authentic texts currently being used in the class.	Review of using context clues and the four-step strategy; student-teacher planning on strategically using and learning more about context clues

Just before showing the video, the teacher passes out the Clue Web shown in Figure 5.2, puts a copy of the Clue Web on the overhead, and tells students that they will use the Clue Web today as they watch the video and over the next few weeks as they learn to use context clues. She goes on to tell them that they probably won't be able to answer all of these questions and should jot down brief answers, while trying to figure out as much as possible about the place described in the video.

At this point, the teacher shows the video, gives students a few minutes to fill in clues on their Clue Web, and then begins a dialogue with them.

Figure 5.2. Clue Web

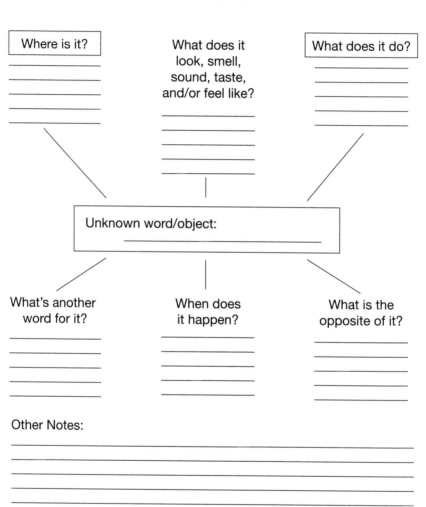

"Was everyone able to get all of the information they needed to answer the questions after watching the video once? Did you catch all that the tour guide said? What would help you figure out even more of the answers?"

Students will almost certainly say that they could learn more if they could watch the tape again. If they don't, the teacher points this out and then replays the video.

After this, she asks for a volunteer to identify the place described in the video, which is Hawaii.

Next, the teacher asks students what clues suggested it was Hawaii. Likely responses include "Hawaiian music," "palm trees," "the beach," and "tropical fruits." The teacher writes these clues on the Clue Web and compliments students on their efforts. Then she challenges them to identify more clues that this is Hawaii and replays the video as many times as students request.

Each time the video is replayed, students record additional clues on their Clue Web and report them to the class. The goal is to demonstrate that the more carefully students watch and the more times they watch, the more clues they can find.

The teacher concludes the introductory lesson by noting that finding all of the clues and figuring out that the place shown in the video was Hawaii required hard work and persistence, that each time they viewed the video again they found more clues, and that this same sort of sleuthing is what they need to do when they are trying to figure out unknown words they meet while reading. She goes on to say that beginning tomorrow they will be learning a particular strategy—a powerful plan—for figuring out the meanings of unknown words they come across. And, she notes, they will find that the strategy is a lot like the approach they used to figure out that the place shown in the video was Hawaii.

Day 2—Introduction to Using Context Clues and the Four-Step Strategy

The teacher begins Day 2 with a brief review of what the class did on Day 1, and then moves quickly to the topic for the day, learning a powerful strategy for figuring out the meanings of unknown words they meet while reading.

"Today, we're going to learn a strategy for using clues to figure something out. But this strategy will not be for figuring out what place is shown in a video. Instead, it will be for figuring out the meanings of unknown words that we meet when we're reading."

"Actually, we won't exactly be 'figuring out' meanings. Instead, we'll be 'inferring meanings.' The strategy is called Inferring Word Meanings from Context. When we infer something, we make an educated guess about it. And when we infer word meanings from context, we are making educated guesses about the meanings of the words. The context in which we find a word doesn't usually tell us the exact meaning of a word, but it often gives us a good idea of the word's meaning, and that is often enough to understand what we are reading."

At this point, the teacher puts up a large and colorful poster with the name of the strategy and its four steps (see sample poster in Figure 5.3) and asks students if they recognize the strategy shown on the poster. A number of students note that they do recognize it, that it is the VCR strategy they worked with the day before.

"Right. This is the same strategy we used yesterday, but now we are applying it to figuring out unknown words we meet in reading rather than to figuring out an unknown place we see in a video. Here's how it works."

"As you can see, the first step in the strategy is Play and Question. That means you read carefully, always asking yourself if you are understanding what you are reading."

"Then, when you come to a word you don't know, you move to the second step—Slow Advance. At this point, you slow down, read the sentence at least once more looking for clues to the meaning of the word, and see if you can infer its meaning."

"If you can infer the word's meaning from just rereading the sentence, that's great. You continue to read. But if you can't infer the word's meaning from reading the sentence, it's time to move to the third step of the strategy—Stop and Rewind. At this point you stop, go back, and read the sentence or two that comes before the one with the unknown word, again looking for clues to the meaning of the word."

"If you can now infer its meaning, excellent. You can move on to the fourth step of the strategy, which is also called Play and

Figure 5.3. Sample Poster Showing Four-Step Strategy for Inferring Word Meanings from Context

---

FOUR-STEP STRATEGY
(Inferring word meanings from context)

1. Play and Question

Read carefully.

Frequently ask yourself, "Does this make sense?"

2. Slow Advance

Notice when you don't know the meaning of a word and slow down.

Read that sentence at least once more, looking for clues.

3. Stop and Rewind

If necessary, go back and reread the preceding sentence, looking for clues that help you figure out what the word might mean.

4. Play and Question

When you figure out what the word might mean, substitute your guess in for the difficult word and see if it makes sense.

If it does, keep on reading.

If it doesn't, stop and rewind, and try again.

Question. But this time Play and Question means to try out the word you inferred. Substitute your educated guess for the word you didn't know and see if that works. If it does, keep on reading. If it doesn't, you'll need to Stop and Rewind again, ask someone about the word, look it up in the dictionary, or simply continue to read, understanding the passage as well as you can without knowing the meaning of the word."

"I know that all of this sounds pretty complicated. And using context clues to infer the meanings of unknown is going to take some work. But the work is well worth it because learning to use context clues helps to make you an independent and powerful reader, a reader who can read anything because you know what to do when unknown words come up. Don't worry if you don't understand the strategy well right now. We are going to spend 2 weeks on it, and together we can master it."

"Now it's time to try out the strategy. And remember, this is just the first of many times we'll do this, and I will be helping you all the way."

Guided Practice. After explaining how to use the four-step strategy for inferring word meanings from context, the teacher and the class work together to infer the meaning of a difficult word. The following teacher-student dialogue is a good example of Guided Practice for the instruction on using context clues.

> *Teacher:* Much like we did with the video, we are going to take a small section of a book and make sure we understand it before moving on. I will read a paragraph aloud and then stop and check to make sure everyone understood the words and the ideas. The book is *The Phantom Tollbooth* by Norton Juster. As you will see, the story is set in a very strange place. Here is the paragraph we're going to work with.
>   "A-H-H-H-R-R-E-M-M," roared the gateman, clearing his throat and snapping smartly to attention. "This is Diction-opolis, a happy kingdom, advantageously located in the Foothills of Confusion. The breezes come right off the Sea of Knowledge and cool the foothills gently. In this kingdom we don't have the cold temperatures like at the top of the mountains, nor the rain that the other side of the mountain gets."
> *Teacher:* This gateman is welcoming the main character, Milo, into his city of Dictionopolis. Notice that Foothills of Confusion and Sea of Knowledge are capitalized. What does that tell you?
> *Students:* They're proper nouns. . . . They're names of places.
> *Teacher:* Exactly. Knowing what sorts of words are capitalized will help you understand this section.
> *Teacher:* Did everyone understand the paragraph completely? If we don't understand everything, what could we do?
> *Students:* Reread it. . . . Read it again. . . . Read it slower. . . . Ask ourselves questions as we are reading it.
> *Teacher:* Good thinking. You came up with two of the steps to our strategy, Slow Advance and Stop and Rewind. Let's use

those two steps now. As I reread the paragraph, listen for words that you don't know.

[*The teacher again reads the paragraph aloud.*]

Teacher: Were there any difficult words in the paragraph? If so, what were they?

Students: Advantageously.

Teacher: Let's highlight that one. Now, let's reread just the sentence that *advantageously* is in and the one after it. We don't need to reread the whole thing every time, just the section we're focusing on.

[*The teacher rereads just the one sentence.*]

Teacher: Does *advantageously* sound like a positive thing?

Students: It does to me. . . . It says that it is a happy kingdom. I think that it has a positive meaning.

Teacher: What are some of the things the paragraph tells us about this kingdom?

Students: That it gets nice breezes off the sea. . . . It's not as cold as the mountain peaks and it's not as rainy as the other side of the mountain.

Teacher: Would that make it a pleasant place to live?

Students: Yes. . . . It's nice to have a breeze. . . . It's also good that it's not too cold. . . . And being not so rainy is a good thing too.

Teacher: What is the word *advantageously* describing?

Students: Where this city is located.

Teacher: That's right. The city is located in an advantageous place. What do you think that *advantageous* could mean?

Students: Nice?

Teacher: Let's add an *-ly* to that because our unknown word had an *-ly.* Then, let's write *nicely* above the word *advantageously.* Now, we should reread the paragraph with our replacement word to see if it makes sense. This time, while I'm reading, ask yourself if you understand what sort of place the story takes place in.

[*The teacher crosses out* advantageously *on the overhead and replaces it with* nicely.]

Teacher: What do you think? Did *nicely* fit in the sentence OK? Does the sentence make sense now?

Students: Yes. . . . It does make sense. . . . Dictionopolis sounds like a good place to live.

Teacher: I agree. I think that we now have a better understanding of the whole paragraph because we understand the word *advantageously* better. That's what learning to use context to infer word meanings can do. It can help us learn words, and it can help us better understand what we read.

Independent Practice. In addition to the Guided Practice illustrated in the teacher-student dialogue, each session from the second day of instruction on includes Independent Practice. This first Independent Practice is brief and does not require the students to do a lot on their own. The teacher gives them a brief paragraph with some difficult words, asks them to read it several times and mark any words they don't know or are uncertain of, and tells them they will discuss using the context clue strategy with this paragraph the next day. As the instruction continues, the Guided Practice portions of the lessons will become much shorter, and the Independent Practice sessions will become longer and more challenging.

Review and Question Session. Each session ends with a review and question session. The teacher reviews what students have learned that day and throughout the unit, primarily by calling on students to recap what they have learned. Each ending session also gives students an opportunity to ask questions and get clarification on anything they are uncertain of.

The Remaining Eight Days of Initial Instruction

As shown in Figure 5.1, over the next 8 days, the class receives detailed instruction on the four-step strategy, interrupts the hard work with a game using the strategy, does guided practice with both narrative text and expository text, uses the strategy with authentic text, and makes plans for using the strategy in the future. There are also several important things that the figure cannot show: Increasingly, the students talk more and the teacher talks less. The students do more of the work. They take more responsibility for the strategy, and they increasingly self-monitor and self-regulate their use of the strategy. At the same time, the teacher is always there to support students' efforts, providing encouragement, scaffolding, and feedback as needed.

Transfer, Review, and Integration Activities

It is vital to realize that this initial unit of using context clues, substantial as it has been, is only the first step in assisting students to become competent and confident users of this important strategy. In the weeks, months, and years after the initial instruction, students need lots of independent practice, feedback, brief reviews and minilessons, opportunities to use the strategy, reminders to use it, and motivation to do so. It is only with such a long-term effort that students will fully learn the strategy, internalize it, and make it a part of their approach to building their vocabularies.

USING WORD PARTS

While using context clues is the most important word-learning strategy, using word parts is a close second. As Nagy, Anderson, Schommer, Scott, and Stallman (1989) have noted, "more than 60% of the new words that readers encounter have relatively transparent morphological structure—that is, they can be broken down into parts" (p. 279). Once words are broken into parts, students can use their knowledge of word parts to attempt to deduce their meanings—if they understand how word parts function. There are three sorts of word parts to consider: prefixes, suffixes, and non-English roots.

Teaching Prefixes

In planning prefix instruction, three preliminary matters deserve consideration: what prefixes to teach, when to teach them, and in what order to teach them. White, Sowell, and Yanagihara (1989) have identified the most frequent prefixes, and these are the ones that should be taught. They are shown in Figure 5.4. As can be seen, these 20 prefixes are used in nearly 3,000 words. Learning them thus provides students with a tremendous resource. Regarding the matter of when to teach them, research (White, Power, & White, 1989) has shown that prefixes are relatively rare in material below the fourth-grade level, and thus the fourth grade is a reasonable time to begin prefix instruction. Finally, with regard to the order in which to teach them, it makes sense to teach the most frequent ones first. All in all, my suggestion is to begin teaching prefixes in the fourth grade and to teach half a dozen or so each year so that the 20 are taught over 3 years. Of course, older students who don't know these 20 most frequent prefixes also need to be taught them.

The instruction outlined here is a one week unit for teaching the first six prefixes. A sample schedule for the unit is shown in Figure 5.5. Additional details of the unit are available in Graves (2004).

Figure 5.4. Twenty Most Frequent Prefixes

Prefix	Words with the Prefix
un-	782
re-	401
in-, im-, ir-, il- (= "not")	313
dis-	216
en-, em-	132
non-	126
in-, im- (= "in," "into")	105
over- (= "too much")	98
mis-	83
sub-	80
pre-	79
inter-	77
fore-	76
de-	71
trans-	47
super-	43
semi-	39
anti-	33
mid-	33
under-	25
total	2,859

Note. Adapted from "Teaching Elementary Students to Use Word-Bit Clues," by T.G. White, J. Sowell, and A. Yanagihara, 1989, *The Reading Teacher, 42.*

Day 1—Introduction, Motivation, and Overview. On Day 1, the teacher introduces the concept of prefixes and the strategy of using prefixes to unlock the meanings of unknown words, attempts to motivate students by stressing the value of prefixes, and gives students an overview of the unit.

Figure 5.5. Overview of a Unit on Prefixes

DAY 1	DAY 2	DAY 3	DAY 4	DAY 5
Introduction, definition of a prefix, motivation to learn to use prefixes, and overview of the unit	Instruction on the first three prefixes using direct explanation	Review and instruction on the prefix strategy	Instruction on the remaining three prefixes and guided practice with the prefix strategy	Review, guided practice, and a quiz

To alert students to what they will be studying and as a continuing reminder throughout the prefix unit, the teacher puts up a poster designed to capture fourth-grade students' attention. At the present time, that might be a poster featuring Spider-Man, with a heading like, "Spider-Man Prefers Prefixes!" and a picture that shows Spider-Man atop a city of prefixes, swinging from one prefix to the next. Then, she might say something like this:

"I think Spider-Man is really on target here. Prefixes are very important and well worth your learning about. This week, we're going to be looking at how you can use prefixes to help you figure out the meanings of words you don't know. If you learn some common prefixes and how to use your knowledge of these prefixes to understand words that contain those prefixes, you're going to be able to figure out the meanings of a lot of new words. And, as you know, figuring out the meanings of words you don't know in a passage is an important step in understanding the passage."

Next, the teacher acknowledges that students probably know some things about prefixes, but notes that it is important that all students have the same information about prefixes and how they work. She then puts up the transparency shown below and reads it to students.

- A prefix is a group of letters that goes in front of a word. *Un-* is one prefix you have probably seen. It often means "not."
- Although you can list prefixes by themselves, as with *un-*, in stories or other things that we read, prefixes are attached to words. They don't appear by themselves. In *unhappy*, for example, the prefix *un-* is attached to the word *happy*.

- When a prefix is attached to a word, it changes the meaning of the word. For example, when the prefix *un-* is attached to the word *happy*, it makes the word *unhappy*, which means "not happy."
- It's important to remember that, for a group of letters to really be a prefix, when you remove them from the word, you still have a real word left. Removing the prefix *un-* from the word *unhappy* still leaves the word *happy*. That means it's a prefix. But if you remove the letters *un* from the word *uncle*, you are left with *cle*, which is not a word. This means that the *un* in *uncle* is not a prefix.

This is a lot for students to remember, so the teacher constructs a shortened version of these points on a Basic Facts About Prefixes poster, puts that up next to the poster advertising the unit, and tells students that the poster will stay up for them to refer to throughout the unit and even after that.

At this point, the teacher asks students if they know any additional prefixes, being generally accepting of their answers, but (assuming that some responses are incorrect) noting that some of the elements they suggested are not actually prefixes and that the class will continue to work on what is and what is not a prefix as the unit progresses.

Finally, the teacher introduces the three prefixes for study the next day—*un-* (not), *re-* (again), and *in-* (not)—putting them on an overhead, asking students to copy them down, and asking students to each bring in a word beginning with one of the prefixes the next day.

Day 2—Instruction on the First Three Prefixes. On Day 2, the teacher uses direct explanation to teach the prefixes *re-*, *un-*, and *in-*. At the beginning of the session, the teacher refers to the "Basic Facts" posters, briefly reminding students what prefixes are, where they appear, and why it is important to know about them. Then the teacher calls on some students to give the prefixed words they have located, jotting those that are indeed prefixed words on the board, and gently noting that the others are not actually prefixed words.

After this, the teacher tells students that today they will be working with the three prefixes introduced the day before and learn how to use them to unlock the meanings of unknown words. The three prefixes are *re-* (meaning "again"), *un-* (meaning "not"), and *in-* (also meaning "not"). In teaching these three prefixes, the teacher will use several types of materials—transparencies introducing each prefix, worksheets with brief exercises requiring use of the prefix just taught, transparencies of these worksheets, exercise sheets requiring additional use and manipulation of each prefix, and review sheets on which students manipulate the three prefixes and the words that were used in illustrating the prefixes for the day. Instruction begins with the teacher displaying the first sentence on the introductory transparency—"Tom was asked to *rewrite* his spelling test because his writing was so messy that the teachers couldn't read it"—and leading students from the meaning of the familiar prefixed word the meaning of the prefix itself as illustrated below:

> *Teacher:* If Tom were asked to rewrite a test, what must he do?
> *Students:* He has to take it over. He has to take it again.
> *Teacher:* That's correct. Using your understanding of the word
>   *rewrite*, what is the meaning of the prefix *re-*?
> *Students:* Again. A second time. Over again.

The process is repeated with three similar sentences on the transparency. After going through these four sentences, the teacher presents a fifth sentence, which defines the unknown root word, and then asks students to define the prefixed word.

After completing this introductory instruction on *re-*, students individually complete review sheets, while a student volunteer completes the review sheet on a transparency. As soon as students complete their review sheets, the volunteer puts the transparency on the overhead so that all students receive immediate feedback on their work. If the volunteer has made an error, the teacher corrects it at this time.

These same procedures are then completed with the two remaining prefixes for the day—*un-* and *in-*. Following initial instruction on the three prefixes, the students complete another review sheet and immediately receive feedback by checking the answers on the back of the sheet.

Day 3—Review and the Prefix Strategy. Day 3 begins with the teacher reviewing the basic facts about prefixes on the Basic Facts About Prefixes poster. Then students complete a review sheet on the three prefixes taught the previous day and immediately correct their work.

Next comes the most crucial part of the instruction—instruction in the prefix strategy. The teacher introduces the strategy by telling students that now that they have worked some with prefixes and understand how useful prefixes can be in figuring out the meanings of unknown words, she is going to teach a specific strategy for working with unknown words. She titles the procedure "Prefix Removal and Replacement," emphasizing that they are using a big name for an important idea.

The teacher then puts up a transparency of the following list, which is reproduced on a prominently displayed Prefix Removal and Replacement Strategy poster, and talks students through the procedure with one or two sample prefixed words.

Prefix Removal and Replacement Strategy

When you come to an unknown word that may contain a prefix:

- Remove the "prefix."
- Check that you have a real word remaining. If you do, you've found a prefix.
- Think about the meaning of the prefix and the meaning of the root word.
- Combine the meanings of the prefix and the root word, and infer the meaning of the unknown word.
- Try out the meaning of the unknown word in the sentence, and see if it makes sense. If it does, read on. If it doesn't, you'll need to use another strategy for discovering the unknown word's meaning.

Following this explicit description of the strategy and modeling of its use, the teacher tells students that they will continue to work on learning the meanings of prefixes and learning to use the strategy over the next few days and in future review sessions. She also reminds them that they now have two posters to refer to when they come to an unknown word that may contain a prefix—the Basic Facts poster and the Prefix Strategy poster. (If the class has a Web site, the posters could also be posted there.)

Day 4—Instruction in the Remaining Three Prefixes and Guided Practice. On Day 4, the teacher teaches the prefixes *dis-, en-,* and *non-* using procedures and materials similar to those used on Day 2. However, on this day, much of the time is spent in guiding students as they use the Prefix Removal and Replacement Strategy. Initially, the teacher provides guidance to the whole class as they use the strategy. Later, students practice using the strategy in pairs, and the teacher provides scaffolding and feedback as needed.

Day 5—Review, Guided Practice, and a Quiz. Day 5 begins with the teacher reviewing the four facts about prefixes, again using the Basic Facts poster in doing so. As part of the review, she asks students a few questions about these facts to be sure they understand them and answers any questions students have.

Next, the teacher reviews the prefix removal and replacement strategy using the "Prefix Strategy" poster. After this, she divides students into small groups and provides guided practice by having the groups use the strategy with the prefixes that have been taught.

As the final activity of the initial instruction, small groups of students work together on a quiz. The quiz requires them to state the four facts about prefixes, state the steps of the prefix removal and replacement strategy, and give the meanings of the six prefixes taught. As soon as students complete the quiz, they correct the quiz in class so that they get immediate feedback on their performance and hand the corrected quizzes in to the teacher so that she has this information on their understanding as she plans reviews.

Transfer, Review, and Integration Activities. As was the case with context clue instruction, initial instruction is only the first step in students' mastering and internalizing the strategy. In the weeks, months, and years after the initial instruction, students need lots of independent practice, feedback, brief reviews and minilessons, opportunities to use the strategy with the texts they are reading, reminders to use it, and motivation to do so.

Instruction in Additional Prefixes and Additional Review and Prompting. As I noted at the beginning of this section, it seems reasonable to teach the 20 most frequent prefixes over a 3-year period. Thus, following the frequency list presented in Figure 5.4, the prefixes *in-* ("in" or "into") through *fore-* might be taught in fifth grade, and the prefixes *de-* through *under-* might be taught in sixth grade. Such instruction would be similar to that used with the initial six prefixes, with one very important exception. Students will have already been taught the basic facts about prefixes and the prefix removal and replacement strategy; work on those matters is review and can be briefer than the initial instruction. Finally, reviewing the information about prefixes and reminding students to make use of prefixes in inferring the meanings of unknown words are still important in the years following initial instruction.

Suffix Instruction

It is important to distinguish two sorts of suffixes: inflectional suffixes and derivational suffixes. Inflectional suffixes have grammatical functions (for example, -*ed* indicating the past tense), while derivational suffixes often have abstract and difficult to explain meanings (for example, -*ence* indicating "the state of being"). The sort of instruction needed is different for these two sorts of suffixes, and it is different for native English speakers than for English learners.

Consider first the matter of inflectional suffixes. Native English speakers already have a tacit understanding of the grammatical functions of inflectional suffixes, and attempting to teach them these grammatical functions is unnecessary and may cause confusion. What native speakers do need is a process for suffix removal, that is, a strategy for mentally separating the suffix from the base word so that they can recognize or decode the base word and then reapply the suffix. White, Sowell, and Yanagihara (1989) describe an excellent procedure for suffix removal. English learners also need the strategy of suffix removal. However, English learners may also need to learn the grammatical functions of inflectional suffixes, that is, they may not know that -*ed* indicates the past tense.

Now consider the matter of derivational suffixes. Because the meanings of many derivational suffixes are abstract and difficult to explain, attempting to teach their meanings is likely to be confusing for elementary students whether they are native speakers or English learners. It seems wise, therefore, to heed the advice that Thorndike (1941) gave over 60 years ago and that White, Sowell, and Yanagihara (1989) more recently endorsed: Some derivational suffixes might be taught to elementary students at opportune times when words containing those suffixes come up in the material students are reading, but systematic instruction in derivational suffixes ought to be reserved for secondary students. As Thorndike suggested, for secondary students "a reasonable amount of deliberate and systematic teaching, if based on adequate knowledge and planned and carried out wisely, can retain [the] merits [of incidental learning], economize time in learning the mother tongue, and give some useful ideas about language" (p. 65).

Non-English Roots

Like suffixes, non-English roots (for example, *anthro* meaning "man" and appearing in such words as *anthropology, misanthrope,* and *philanthropy*) represent a very different teaching and learning situation than do prefixes. I do not recommend systematic instruction in non-English roots for several reasons: There are a large number of non-English roots; individual roots are not used in anywhere near the number of words common prefixes are used in; they are often variously spelled and thus difficult to identify; and the relationship between the original meaning of the root and the current meaning of the English word in which it is used is often vague. However, teachers may want to provide some incidental instruction in roots, particularly for secondary students. That is, if certain roots come up repeatedly in the material students are reading—as might be the case in a science class—then teaching these roots is likely to be worthwhile. Also, if older students want to learn non-English roots as part of their "personal approach to building vocabulary," a topic I discuss later in this chapter, they should certainly be encouraged to do so. Additionally, teachers may want to teach students about the fact that many English words are derived from non-English roots as part of promoting their word conscious, a topic I discuss in Chapter 6.

USING THE DICTIONARY AND RELATED REFERENCE TOOLS

Teaching students to use the dictionary and related reference tools is a much smaller task than is teaching the use of context clues or word parts. Nevertheless, it is to students' advantage to become effective and efficient in using these tools. As Miller and Gildea (1987) have convincingly demonstrated, students frequently have difficulty using the dictionary to define unknown words. For example, after looking up the meaning of *meticulous* and finding the phrase "very careful" in its definition, one student employed the new word in a sentence that read "I was meticulous about falling off the cliff." Obviously, this student found at least some dictionary definitions considerably less than helpful. Perhaps this should not be surprising. Students often receive instruction in alphabetizing, in using guide words, and in using pronunciation keys. However, instruction usually does not go much beyond this, and such instruction is not sufficient for teaching students to effectively work with a tool that they will use throughout their schooling and that most adults continue to keep nearby for reference.

The starting point for helping students become effective and efficient dictionary users is getting them the right level of dictionary. Primary-grade students need dictionaries designed for the primary grades, upper elementary students need dictionaries designed for those grades, and so on. Once students have appropriate dictionaries, the instruction parallels that for context clues and word parts, although it is not nearly as lengthy as that instruction.

As is the case with teaching the use of context clues and word parts, motivation, an explanation of what they are going to be working on, and the use of guidelines, modeling, and the gradual release of responsibility provide a powerful approach. Perhaps a week or so before the instruction begins, you could post this question on the board: "What book appears in every classroom, every library, and many people's homes?" On the first day of instruction, take students' responses in writing, tally them, and report the results. In all probability, most students will answer the question correctly, and you can congratulate them. Whether or not most answer correctly, note that the answer is "the dictionary," and stress that it is a very important book indeed. Then, tell students that you are going to be working on using the dictionary to define words, that spending some time learning to use the dictionary is worthwhile, and that using the dictionary sometimes isn't as simple as it seems. Next, put some guidelines like those shown in the list below on a bulletin board and leave them up over the upcoming weeks. Here, I have phrased the guidelines for middle or secondary school students. For younger students, they could be phrased more simply.

- When reading a definition, be sure to read all of it, not just part of it.
- Remember that many words have more than one meaning.
- Be sure to check all the definitions the dictionary gives for a word, not just one of them.
- Decide which definition makes sense in the passage in which you found the word.
- Often the dictionary works best when you already have some idea of a word's meaning. This makes the dictionary particularly useful for checking on a word you want to use in your writing.

The teacher does not have students memorize these guidelines, but talks through them, amplifying them as necessary. For example, she should probably add to the third guideline by telling students that if they find that they still know nothing about an important word after considering context, looking for words parts, and checking the dictionary, they will probably want to ask someone about its meaning. Similarly, she might want to add to the last guideline by noting that one of the most frequent uses of the dictionary, whether for reading or for writing, is to confirm, clarify, or refute the meaning they have arrived at using context or a meaning they are only somewhat confident in.

The remainder of the procedure continues to parallel that used with context and word parts. The teacher does some modeling to demonstrate how to look up the meaning of an unknown word. She thinks aloud, sharing her thinking with students as she comes across the unknown

stigma example

word in a text. She shows students how she looks through the dictionary and finds the word, finds the definition that seems to fit, considers all of that definition, and then mentally checks to see if the meaning she chooses makes sense in the context in which the unknown word occurred. Gradually students should take over the procedure and model it for the teacher and for each other. Students should be encouraged to use the procedure when they come across unknown or vaguely known words in context. Finally, from time to time, students should be given opportunities to model their thinking as they use the dictionary so that the teacher can check their proficiency and give them feedback and further instruction as needed.

In addition to learning this general approach to using a dictionary, students need to learn some things about the particular dictionary they use—what the entries for individual words contain and how they are arranged, what aids to its use the dictionary provides, and what features beyond the basic word list the dictionary includes. Much of the important information appears in the front matter of the dictionaries themselves, but it is very seldom read, and simply asking students to read it is hardly sufficient instruction. Thus explicit instruction in how to use specific dictionaries is usually useful.

Additionally, students need to be made aware of computerized dictionaries, taught how to use them, and be convinced that they are worth using. The word processor I am currently using—Microsoft Word X for Mac (Microsoft Corp., 2001)—contains a huge dictionary that I access repeatedly as I write and edit. It provides concise definitions, parts of speech, some information on level of formality, and spelling—in seconds and without leaving the computer. While this particular electronic dictionary is most appropriate for secondary students, word processors for younger students typically have simpler, age-appropriate dictionaries.

Students also need instruction in using the thesaurus. Specific attention to the thesaurus is worthwhile because the thesaurus is used for a somewhat different purpose than is the dictionary. In general, the dictionary is used when a word has already been identified—when you have read it and want to be certain of its meaning or when you are considering using it in writing and want to check its meaning or its spelling. A thesaurus, on the other hand, is much more likely to be used when you are looking for a word to use. A thesaurus is useful when you have something to say but want a new way of saying it. Getting students in the habit of using a thesaurus is a step toward getting them to enlarge their active vocabularies as well as a step toward getting them interested in words.

As is the case with the dictionary, students need to be made aware of, sold on, and taught how to use a computerized thesaurus. Many word processing programs also contain very useful thesauri. Microsoft Word X for Mac comes with an integrated thesaurus that enables me to easily replace a word in a text I am working on with a related synonym. Students who would rarely—possibly never—take a thesaurus off the bookshelf to find a more powerful or more appropriate word to use in their writing will readily use an electronic thesaurus.

Two other types of dictionaries are useful for English learners: dictionaries specifically designed for English learners and dictionaries of idioms. *Collins COBUILD New Student's Dictionary* (2002) is an excellent example of a dictionary that can be helpful for English learners. It both defines words in common, easy to understand language and gives a sample sentence for each word. For example, the definition for furious is "If someone is furious, they are extremely angry," and the sample sentence is "He was furious at the way his wife had been treated" (p. 283). *Longman American Idioms Dictionary* (1999) is a good example of a very usable dictionary of idioms. It provides helpful definitions for over 4,000 idioms. Here, for example, is the entry for *the buck stops here:* "used to say that you are the person who is responsible for something that needs to be dealt with: *I think the captain knows that the buck stops with him and that he'll have to take responsibility*" (p. 41).

DEVELOPING A STRATEGY FOR DEALING WITH UNKNOWN WORDS

In addition to learning to use context cues, word parts, and various types of dictionaries, students will profit from having some plans for what to do when they encounter an unknown word as they are reading. My advice is to give them a definite strategy, discuss the strategy with them, let them try it out, and then discuss how it worked and how they might modify it to fit their specific needs. Here are the steps for the strategy as you might initially list them on an overhead or the board.

1. Recognize that an unknown word has occurred.
2. Decide whether you need to understand it to understand the passage.
3. Attempt to infer the meaning of the word from the context surrounding it.

4. Attempt to infer the meaning looking for word parts.
5. Attempt to sound out the word and see if you come up with a word you know.
6. Turn to a dictionary, glossary, or another person for the meaning.

The initial instruction here could be completed in a half hour or so. Then, students should use the strategy for a few days. After that, it is appropriate to discuss how it worked for students and to bring up the matter of modifying the strategy so that it best fits their needs. Finally, from time to time, briefly review the strategy and ask students how their approaches to dealing with unknown words they encounter are working and what suggestions they may have to share with the class.

ADOPTING A PERSONAL APPROACH
TO BUILDING VOCABULARY

As already noted, because of the size of the vocabulary learning task students face, we want to promote a rich variety of approaches to learning words. One of them is to have students individually commit themselves to an approach that they will use. Many approaches can be beneficial. What is important is that students consciously recognize that building their vocabularies is important and make some sort of personal commitment to learning words. Having such a personal commitment is, of course, particularly important for English learners, who often face a massive vocabulary learning task. Listed here are some alternatives, a list you can add to as you work with students and elicits their suggestions.

- Make a commitment to learn a word a day, from almost any source.
- Make a commitment to learn a word or two a week. (For some students, a word a day may be too much.)
- Identify a particular prefix or suffix, or perhaps a Latin or Greek root, and learn and use words containing those word parts over a period of a month or so, probably compiling a list of those words.
- Decide to become a real sleuth at using context and agree to learn at least two or three new words each week from context and to record both the words learned and the context from which they were learned.
- Routinely use the thesaurus when writing and keep a journal of the words originally used and the words that replaced them.

The basic approach is to present these alternatives on an overhead or the board and discuss them with students. In this activity, be particularly attentive to drawing out students' suggestions. Then, in closing the discussion, attempt to secure a vocabulary-learning commitment from each student. Initially, you might ask for a month's commitment. During the month, check periodically to see how students' approaches are working and give them feedback and encouragement. Then, at the end of the month, hold another discussion on the matter. At that time, try to decide whether individual students should continue with the approach to independent word learning they have been using or perhaps try another approach. It is probably worth considering that having an approach is probably more important than what exactly that approach is.

WHEN SHOULD THE STRATEGIES BE TAUGHT?

Obviously, teaching all of the strategies described in this chapter is not the responsibility of a single teacher or something that can be done in a single year. Exactly what is taught when and who is responsible for the instruction will differ from school to school and will depend on what instruction students have had in the past. Here, however, are some suggestions. During the primary-grade years, keep things simple and informal. The in-depth teaching procedures described here become appropriate at about the fourth-grade level. Prior to that, short and informal minilessons should be sufficient. The one procedure that needs to be taught formally during the primary grades is suffix removal, which is actually a decoding procedure. Two strategies that should not be taught in the primary grades are using prefixes and using root words, in both cases because these elements are not frequent enough in primary-grade material to justify the time it takes to teach them.

Grades 4 through 6 are when most of the more formal instruction should take place. Because using context is the most valuable word-learning strategy, it should probably be taught first, that is, in Grade 4. Using prefixes is the next most valuable strategy and should be taught next. If time permits, that instruction should probably begin in fourth grade; if not, it can wait till fifth grade. Whenever prefix instruction begins, it should probably be extended over 3 years, beginning with the most frequent half dozen or so prefixes in the first year and teaching another half dozen or so in the each of the next 2 years. Teaching students to use the dictionary and related reference tools, develop a strategy for dealing with unknown words, and develop a personal approach to building vocabulary are much shorter endeavors. These can be taught whenever you decide that students need them. Regardless of when the strategies are initially taught, they need to be reviewed; students need to be reminded about them, and students need to be prompted to use them in the years following initial instruction.

If all of the strategies are taught well in Grades 1–6, then the main tasks left for Grades 7–12 are reviewing, prompting, and encouraging. In the best of all worlds, though, this would not be left to chance. That is, reviewing certain word-learning strategies at certain times would be specified in the curriculum. One target of instruction that remains for the secondary grades is that of Latin and Greek roots. When a Latin or Greek root shows itself to be useful in a particular content area—science, history, and so on—it should probably be taught. Also, if any of the five strategies have not been taught well in the earlier grades, then they need to be taught well in the secondary grades. Given what we know about the vocabulary instruction that currently takes place in school, it will frequently be the case that they have not been taught well in the earlier grades and need to be taught in these later grades.

CONCLUDING REMARKS

The purpose of this chapter has been to describe a general approach to teaching word-learning strategies and then to give detailed procedures for teaching students five powerful strategies: Using context; using word parts; using the dictionary and related reference tools; developing a strategy for dealing with unknown words; and adopting a personal approach to building vocabulary.

Throughout the chapter, I have tried to show that strategy instruction should be begin with direct explanation but then become increasingly transactional—constructivist, flexible, and imbedded in the ongoing curriculum—over time. Transactional instruction is difficult to show in print, a very static medium. Consequently, I conclude this chapter with a list showing some of the transactional aspects of strategy instruction, some end points you want to arrive at with students. The list relies a good deal upon suggestions from Brown and Campione (1990) and Pressley, Harris, and Marks (1992).

- The teacher and the students interact, with modeling, scaffolding, and discussion prominent.
- Children assume the role of *active* participants.

- It is understood that the knowledge the teacher has cannot be transmitted directly to the students.
- There is considerable discussion and debate.
- Teachers frequently make on-the-spot diagnoses of individual students' understanding and progress.
- The instruction proceeds at a rate and sequence that is dictated by the students' needs and progress.
- Understanding is emphasized as strategies are developed.
- Students are always informed about the purposes of the strategies taught.
- Developing students' self-monitoring and self-regulation skills are central concerns.

CHAPTER 6

Promoting Word Consciousness

Word consciousness—and especially understanding the power of word choice—is essential for sustained vocabulary growth. Words are the currency of written language. Learning new words is an invest-ment, and students will make the required investment to the extent that they believe that the investment is worthwhile.

Judith Scott and William Nagy, Vocabulary Scholars

W ords are indeed the "currency of written language," as Scott and Nagy so nicely put it. Moreover, as Scott and Nagy also note, students are likely to make the required investment needed to learn vocabulary only if they believe that the investment is worthwhile. Thus one of the major long-term goals of vocabulary in-struction is to assist students to gain a deep appreciation of words and to value them, a goal that has been termed *word consciousness*. Sim-ply stated, word consciousness refers to *awareness of* and *interest in* words and their meanings. As defined by Anderson and Nagy (1992), word consciousness involves both a cognitive and an affective stance toward words. Word consciousness integrates metacognition about words, motivation to learn words, and deep and lasting interest in words.

Students who are word conscious are aware of the words around them—those they read and hear and those they write and speak. This awareness involves an appreciation of the power of words, an understand-ing of why certain words are used instead of others, and a sense of the words that could be used in place of those selected by a writer or speaker. It also involves, as Scott and Nagy (2004) emphasize, recognition of the communicative power of words, of the differences between spoken and written language, and of the particular importance of word choice in written language. And it involves an interest in learning and using new words and becoming more skillful and precise in word usage.

The process of acquiring vocabulary is complex, and for many stu-dents acquiring the rich store of words that will help them succeed in and beyond school is a challenge. With tens of thousands of words to learn and with most of this word learning taking place incidentally as students are reading and listening, a positive disposition toward words is crucial to students' success in expanding the breadth and depth of their word knowledge over the course of their lifetime. Word consciousness exists at many levels of complexity and sophistication, and can and should be fostered among preschoolers as well as among students in and beyond high school.

Two factors, both of which I have already discussed, argue for the importance of word consciousness. First, there is the growing realization that for all learners—from primary-grade children to college students—motivation and affect are every bit as important to learning as cognition (see, National Research Council, 2004; Pressley et al., 2003; Wigfield & Eccles, 2002). Word consciousness is the motivational and affective component of the multifaceted vocabulary program described in this book. Second, there is the increasing evidence that lack of vocabulary is a key factor underlying school failure for disadvantaged students (Becker, 1977; Biemiller, 2004; Chall et al., 1990; Hart & Risley, 1995). Kindling students' interest and engagement with words is a vital part of helping all students, but especially less advantaged students, to develop rich and powerful vocabularies. The National Research Council (2004) sums up the cost of disengagement for less advantaged students particularly well: "When students from advantaged backgrounds become disengaged, they may learn less than they could, but they usually get by or they get second chances; most eventually graduate and move on to other opportunities. In contrast, when students from disadvantaged . . . backgrounds become disengaged, they . . . face severely limited opportunities" (p. 1).

In this chapter, I discuss a number of specific approaches to fostering word consciousness in all students and in a variety of contexts—in reading, in writing, and in discussion. They include

- Modeling, Recognizing, and Encouraging Adept Diction
- Promoting Word Play
- Providing Rich and Expressive Instruction
- Involving Students in Original Investigations
- Teaching Students about Words.

In general, the approaches are arranged from those that are less informal and less time consuming to those that are more formal, more time consuming, and more demanding on the learner, although this is not a hard and fast progression.

MODELING, RECOGNIZING, AND
ENCOURAGING ADEPT DICTION

Modeling adept diction, recognizing skillful diction in the texts students are reading, and constantly encouraging students to employ adept diction in their own speech and writing are starting points in building word consciousness. As with teaching in general, modeling is critical. Specifically, it is vital to model both enthusiasm for and proficiency in adept word usage.

Consider the difference between asking a student to close the door because it is *not quite closed* and asking him to close the door because it is *ajar*, the difference between describing the color in a student's painting as *greenish-yellow* as opposed to *chartreuse*, or the difference between describing Tiger Woods as an *excellent* athlete or a *consummate* athlete. When students hear unfamiliar words used to describe concepts they are familiar with and care about, they become curious about the world of words. In addition, they learn—from experience— that word choice possibilities are immense and varied. As their "word worlds" open up, so too do the wider worlds in which they live.

Another opportunity to model, recognize, and encourage adept diction is to use the tried-and-true word-of-the-day approach. Allocating time each day to examine a new word can be effective with students of all ages. The word can be teacher-selected or student-selected and might be chosen from books, magazine articles, or newspapers, or from heard contexts such as appropriate television programs, discussions, and other teachers. It often works well to begin with teacher-selected words and to present the word and its meaning, including both definitional and contextual information, an explanation of why it was selected, and examples of how it relates to the lives of one or more members of the class. When appropriate, adding relevant pictures, gestures, concrete objects, and drama increases students' enthusiasm and understanding. Further, a period for student questions and comments allows for the type of deep processing necessary for effective word learning (Stahl, 1998).

Scott and her colleagues (1996) have studied vocabulary as a vehicle for connecting reading and writing. Within the context of literature discussion groups, they assign one student the role of word hunter, whose job it is to look for particularly interesting uses of language in the literature read by the group. This student might, for example, draw the group's attention to Sharon Creech's use of the word *lunatic* in *Walk Two Moons* (1994) to describe a mysterious stranger. Why doesn't the author use *mentally ill* or *weirdo?* How does the author's word choice relate to the character who first uses the word to describe the mysterious fellow? Such discussions can lead students to more thoughtful word choices in their own writing.

Another way to encourage adept diction in students' writing and speaking is to scaffold their use of new words. They might construct *sensory webs* for words likely to be useful in their writing or for words they have read and would like to understand more fully. The lines leading from the word itself outward provide places for students to fill in what the word smells like, tastes like, looks like, sounds like, and feels like. Scott and her colleagues (1996), for example, report that one of the sixth graders they worked with wrote that *anger* smells like "hot burning coals," looks like "shattered glass on the pavement," tastes like "dry sand burning in the desert," sounds like "fingernails screeching on the blackboard," and feels like "a cold wind gripping you all over." Figure 6.1 shows this student's responses along with some additional ones.

A related technique used by Scott and her colleagues (1996) to help students expand the word choices used in their writing is to have students brainstorm words related to a key word. For the word *anxious*, one student came up with the related words *shaky, fidgeting, worried, apprehensive, nervous,* and *impatient.*

Of course, attention to word choices is as important for older writers as it is for younger ones—for middle school, high school, and adult writers. For me, checking word choices is almost always my last step in honing a piece of writing to best convey my message and fit my audience.

Figure 6.1. Sensory Web for *Anger*

Looks Like
shattered glass on the pavement
a hurricane making landfall

Smells Like	*Feels Like*
hot burning coals	a cold wind
a huge forest fire	you've been in a fist fight
racing toward you	

ANGER

Tastes Like	*Sounds Like*
dry sand	fingernails on a blackboard
chili peppers	raccoons screeching in the dark

PROMOTING WORD PLAY

One of the primary goals of beginning reading instruction is to teach and reinforce the notion that printed words convey meaning. But words do much more than convey meaning. Words and phrases can simultaneously feel good on the tongue, sound good to the ear, and incite a riot of laughter in the belly. Verbal phenomena such as homophones and homographs; idioms, clichés, and puns; and onomastics (the story of names) offer myriad opportunities for investigating language. And word play books and other interesting books about words are available for children of all ages, as well as for adults. Students of all ages get real pleasure out of words that sound alike, words that look alike, and words that look nothing like what they mean.

Moreover, it needs to be emphasized that word play is not a frill. As Blachowicz and Fisher (2004) explain, it is an activity firmly grounded in sound pedagogy and in research:

- Word play calls on students to reflect metacognitively on words, word parts, and context.
- Word play requires students to be active learners and capitalizes on possibilities for the social construction of meaning.
- Word play develops domains of word meaning and relatedness as it engages students in practice and rehearsal of words. (p. 219)

Homophones and Homographs

Homophones present many opportunities for enjoyment and learning. Children delight in images such as those of a "towed toad," a "sail sale," or a "Sunday sundae." One activity that many children enjoy is drawing such homophone pairs, and one approach that has proven useful is to have students fold a piece of drawing paper into quadrants so they can write homophone pairs in the boxes on the left side of the paper and draw corresponding pictures in the boxes on the right side of the paper. Games such as Homophone Bingo and Homophone Concentration offer additional possibilities for experimenting with homophones.

Some words, of course, not only sound alike, but are spelled alike—and still have more than one meaning. In fact, a large proportion of English words have more than one meaning. These homographs allow for a variety of games, including the following one, taken from Richard Lederer's *Get Thee to a Punnery* (1988), a word-play book for adults. In each of the lines below, students insert a word that means the same as the word or phrase at either end; the number of blanks indicates the number of letters in the missing word.

- summit __ __ __ spinning toy (top)
- hole __ __ __ fruit stone (pit)
- nation __ __ __ __ __ __ rural area (country)

Having students complete such puzzles can be fun and entertaining, but having them create such items can be even more valuable. As with many word-play activities, making up items of this sort is well within the reach of many children and provides an active, creative, and rewarding learning experience.

Idioms, Clichés, and Puns

Children are often fascinated by idioms such as "A bird in the hand is worth two in the bush" and "Don't count your chickens until they're hatched." Representing as they do the language of particular groups, idioms reflect particular periods of time, particular regions of the country, and particular cultures. Children can enjoy drawing or dramatizing the literal meanings of idioms such as "Don't look a gift horse in the mouth," "Roll with the punches," and "food for thought" and contrasting them with their figurative meanings. On a different note, remember that idioms can present a particular problem to English learners. Because the literal meanings of the words don't apply, students just learning English may find them incomprehensible and thus confusing. It is important, then, to be on the lookout for potentially troublesome idioms and clarify their meaning for English learners. The *Longman American Idioms Dictionary* (1999) provides a listing of over 4,000 of them.

Clichés are often thought of as being unimaginative and trite. But in fact they are examples of language use that has endured over time, expressing timeless sentiments and wisdom. They are at once familiar phrases and expressions of shared human experience, making them accessible and important forms of language for students to experience. Teachers can kindle students' word awareness by being "down to earth" with them, warning them about "jumping out of the frying pan into the fire," and repeatedly playing around with phrases such as these "until the cows come home."

Like clichés, puns are memorable and often quite clever. Advertisers feature them in songs and jingles, noted authors make use of them, and newspapers frequently employ them in headlines. In *Romeo and Juliet,* for example, the dying Mercutio can't resist a pun as he exclaims,

"Look for me tomorrow, and you will find me a grave man." The day after the Minnesota Vikings' star kicker muffed a short field goal that led to the team's ouster from the playoffs, the *Minneapolis Star-Tribune* ran the headline "Kicked Out!" And even the prestigious *New York Times* employs them from time to time, as seen in this line, "Balloons have become a high flying business and sell at inflated prices."

Onomastics

Onomastics, the study of names, is yet another form of word play, one that Johnson, Johnson, and Schlichting (2004) have examined in some depth. Words derive their names from various sources; you can use your knowledge of these sources in two ways. First, you can occasionally mention the derivation of a name as part of the overall attempt to raise students' word consciousness. Second, you can explain one or more of the various sources of words and let students search for words derived in those various ways. For example, *eponyms* are words named after people. The Sequoia redwood is named after Chief Sequoya (1770?–1843), the Geiger counter after Hans Geiger (1882–1945), and beef Wellington after the 1st Duke of Wellington (1759–1852). Students can look up these historical figures and learn just what they did to warrant having their names become a permanent part of our language. Alternately, you might give students words that are derived from people's names and ask students to trace the story behind them. Some examples Johnson and his colleagues suggest are *cobb salad, maverick, frisbee,* and *Tony Award.*

As another example, some names, which Johnson and his colleagues term *aptronyms,* are particularly appropriate for a person's profession. They located a Doctor Smart, who is a professor, a family named Woods, who own a lumber yard, and a Ms. Carb, who manages a bakery; and my wife once had a surgeon named *Les Sharp.* Students enjoy making up aptronyms for people in various professions, such as Ruth Decay or Dennis Drill for dentists. These are just two of a number of forms of onomastics Johnson and his colleagues discuss, along with other sorts of word play including expressions, figures of speech, word associations, word formations, word manipulations, word games, and ambiguities. All are worth considering.

Word-Play Books

A wide array of books lend themselves to raising word consciousness and to teaching a host of interesting facts about words. Books are available for every age and grade level, and they deal with many aspects of words. There are alphabet books, books that include extensive word play, books in which words play a central role, books about word play, books filled with word games, books about the history of words, books of proverbs, books about slang, and books about nearly any other aspect of words you could think of. The county library I use—which I would characterize as a medium-size library—lists over 150 books under the term "words." A search on the Amazon Web site with the term "word books" yielded 101,064 items. (A careful search of the Amazon search results would reveal that not all of those books are the sort of books I'm describing here, but a lot of them are.) My point is that there are far more word and word-play books than I can possibly describe here. Consequently, I am listing one book in each of several categories to suggest the range of books available, but I encourage you to check your local library, your local bookstore, as well as Internet sources such as amazon.com and barnesandnoble.com for many more titles.

Two wonderful alphabet books are Graeme Base's *Animalia* (1986) and Judith Vorst's *The Alphabet from Z to A (with Much Confusion on the Way)* (1994). Each combines clever illustrations with inviting text and appeals to both young and highly sophisticated readers. Where else but in a book like *Animalia* can you find "crafty crimson cats carefully catching crusty crayfish"?

Two books that highlight the richness of language are Fred Gwynne's *The King Who Rained* (1970) and Louis Sachar's *Holes* (1998), which won the 1999 Newberry Medal. The first revolves around words with multiple meanings, and the second is filled with interesting words, some of which provide clues to the central puzzle of the novel, and others which, like Stanley Yelnats, the palindrome name of the protagonist, are simply fun.

Two books whose plots center around words and language are Norton Juster's *The Phantom Tollbooth* (1961) and Andrew Clements's *Frindle* (1996). Juster's book describes Milo's adventures in the fantasy world of Dictionopolis, where rich and interesting words make their home. Clements's novel tells the story of Nick, who invents the word *frindle*, convinces kids in his school to use it instead of the word *pen*, and watches as his word spreads to the city, the nation, the world, and even the dictionary.

Two word play books are Richard Lederer's *Pun and Games* (1996), intended for middle-grade students, and *Get Thee to a Punnery* (1988), intended for adults but also appropriate for high school students. *Pun and Games* includes, as recorded in the subtitle, "jokes, riddles, daffynitions, tairy fales, rhymes, and more word play for kids," while *Get Thee to a Punnery* contains lots of puns but also some challenging word games. Additionally, Blachowicz and Fisher's "Keep the 'Fun' in Fundamental" (2004) provides dozens of word-play activities as well as sources for still more activities.

Finally, two books about words and language appropriate for teachers are Greenman's *Words That Make a Difference—and How to Use Them in a Masterly Way* (2000), and Pinker's *The Language Instinct* (2000). Almost all of *Words That Make a Difference* is exactly what a vocabulary book is not supposed to be—an alphabetical list of words and their definitions. But two things save it from being a bad book and make it a very good one. Accompanying each word and definition is a short passage from the *New York Times* in which a writer used the word in a clever, memorable, and appropriate way. Additionally, the words are at just the right level of difficulty—ones that we have heard but don't use because we are not quite sure of them—and many are appropriate for stretching high school students' vocabularies. *The Language Instinct*, on the other hand, is very much what a book about language directed at a general audience ought to be. In it, Pinker, an eminent MIT linguist, gives his theories about the nature, origin, and development of language. Although not all agree with Pinker, the book is definitely interesting, exciting, accessible, and filled with ideas to share with students. *Publishers Weekly* called it "a beautiful hymn to the infinite creative potential of language."

PROVIDING RICH AND EXPRESSIVE INSTRUCTION

In keeping with the plan for this chapter to present less formal and less time-consuming activities earlier, the first activity described in this section—Scott and her colleagues' (Scott et al., 1994; Scott & Nagy, 2004) technique for encouraging students to incorporate more interesting and sophisticated vocabulary into their writing—is the less formal and less time-consuming activity. The next two activities—Beck and McKeown's Rich Instruction and Duin's Expressive Instruction (Beck et al., 1982; McKeown & Beck, 2004; Duin & Graves, 1987, 1988)—are more deliberately structured and more time-consuming.

The basic logic underlying Scott's program is this: Reading and writing are reciprocal processes. Significant word learning—and, I would say, the opportunity to develop word consciousness—requires children to be immersed in situations in which rich, precise, interesting, and inventive use of words is valued. Such an environment is created by employing quality children's literature that contains rich, precise, interesting, and inventive use of words; encouraging students to identify these apt and creative uses of language; and honoring these words and phrases by posting them prominently around the room and frequently calling students' attention to them. Thus Scott immerses students in good children's literature, encourages them to select words and phrases they value, and has them post these words and phrases in the classroom. She then encourages students to "borrow" the words and phrases they have identified in their reading and use the words in their writing. Next, she designs writing activities that encourage use of rich and varied vocabulary and suggests that students "catch" the words and phrases on the board, modify them to fit the subjects they're writing about, and use these modifications of professional writers' phrasing in their own writing.

One of the books the children read, enjoyed, and found many interesting words and phrases in was Natalie Babbitt's *Tuck Everlasting* (1975). A number of words and phrases from *Tuck* were copied and posted around the classroom, and a number of students were able to incorporate these in their writing. For example, one of the phrases from *Tuck* that a student decided to use was "a great potato of a woman." In the student's writing, this phrase became "a long string bean of a man," an interesting transformation and a very vivid image.

Another and more elaborate borrowing came from the following paragraph of Babbitt's novel:

> "So," said Tuck to himself. "Two years. She's been gone two years." He stood up and looked around, embarrassed, trying to clear the lump from his throat. But there was no one to see him. The cemetery was very quiet. In the branches of the willow behind him, a red-winged blackbird chirped. Tuck wiped his eyes hastily. Then he straightened his jacket again and drew up his hand in a brief salute. "Good girl," he said aloud. And then he turned and left the cemetery, walking slowly. (p. 138)

Recast by a student, the prose was transformed into this poem.

In Loving Memory
Winifred Foster
Jackson
Dear Wife
Dear Mother
1870–1948
"So," said Tuck to himself
gone two years
Embarrassed
clear the lump from his throat

Quiet cemetery
Black bird chirped
Wiped his eyes
"Good girl," he said out loud
Quickly departed
Sadness filled the air.
—Kirn (Scott et al., 1994, p. 43)

We think it is especially noteworthy that in activities such as these, students are both learning something about vocabulary and learning something about, and perhaps coming to appreciate, the author's craft.

I described in Chapter 4 how Beck and McKeown's Rich Instruction and Duin's Expressive Instruction can be used to teach individual words. Here, I describe how they can be used for fostering word consciousness. Since the two include similar activities, I describe them together. The first step is to select a small set of words that are semantically related. One set used by Beck and McKeown—*rival, hermit, novice, virtuoso, accomplice, miser, tyrant,* and *philanthropist*—contains words that refer to people. A set used by Duin—*advocate, capability, tether, criteria, module, envision, configuration, and quest*—contains words that can be used in talking about space exploration.

The next step, the central part of the instruction, is to have students work extensively and intensively with the words, spending perhaps half an hour a day over a period of a week or so with them, and engaging in a dozen or so diverse activities with them—really getting to know them, discovering their shades of meaning and the various ways in which they can be used, and realizing what interesting companions words can be. Beck and McKeown's activities, for example, included asking students to respond to words like *virtuoso* and *miser* with thumbs up or thumbs down to signify approval or disapproval; asking which of three actions an *accomplice* would be most likely to engage in—robbing a bank by himself, stealing some candy, or driving a getaway car; and asking such questions as Could a *virtuoso* be a *rival?* Could a *virtuoso* be a *novice?* and Could a *philanthropist* be a *miser?* Duin's activities included asking students to discuss how *feasible* space travel might soon be, asking them how a space station could *accommodate* handicapped persons, and asking them to write brief essays called "Space Shorts" in which they used the words in dealing with such topics as the foods that might be available in space.

The third step, which was used only in Duin's Expressive Instruction, is to have students write more extensive essays using as many of the taught words as possible, playing with them and exploring their possibilities. Duin's students appeared to really enjoy this activity. As their teacher observed, "Students who were asked to write often and use the words in written class work showed great involvement in their writing" (p. 327). The students also showed that they could indeed use the new words adroitly. One student, for example, noted that "the space program would be more *feasible* if we sent more than just astronauts and satellites into space" and then suggested that designers should "change the whole *configuration* of the space shuttle so that it could *accommodate* more people" (p. 328).

Finally, I would add a fourth step, directly discussing with students the word choices they make, why they make those choices, and how adroit use of words makes speech and writing more precise, more memorable, and more interesting. Note that when either Rich Instruction or Expressive Instruction is used for the purpose of fostering word consciousness, the main goal is to get students involved with and excited about words. Using these clever and intriguing approaches several times a year should be a substantial contribution to reaching this goal.

INVOLVING STUDENTS IN ORIGINAL INVESTIGATIONS

The activities described in the previous sections call students' attention to words in various ways, some of which are more deliberate than others. This section addresses the role of still more systematic efforts—research conducted by students themselves—in the development of word consciousness. Such original investigations centered on vocabulary provide a wealth of opportunities for increasing word consciousness. An array of options for investigations exist, some centered on text, some on speech, and some on interviews of language users.

Investigations focusing on written text are particularly doable because the data sources are readily available. One option, appropriate for secondary students, is to investigate the vocabulary used in various texts. For example, students might compare the typical number of words in articles in *USA Today* and the *New York Times*. As part of such a study, they could use some metric of word difficulty to examine the differential difficulty of the vocabulary in the two papers, perhaps tallying words beyond the first 10,000 most frequent in *The Educator's Word Frequency Guide* (Zeno et al., 1995). Such a study could lead to fruitful discussions of why those differences exist, as well as a discussion of the reading process and text features associated with lower and higher levels of text difficulty.

Investigations of spoken language are somewhat more difficult because the language must be recorded before it can be analyzed. One source of spoken language that is readily accessible is television. Middle-grade students might enjoy analyzing the vocabulary used in cartoons, looking perhaps for colorful adjectives used by the characters. Similarly, secondary students might enjoy comparing the terminology used in police dramas, medical series, news broadcasts, and other types of programs. More demanding tasks might involve recording language use in natural settings. I can still remember a really interesting study of the speech of short order cooks done by a University of Minnesota student 20 years ago. In a similar vein, students could work in small groups to study vocabulary use within particular contexts such as the school cafeteria, the gym during basketball practice, or places where they work. Students with very young siblings might record 10 minutes or so of talk a week over a period of a month and draw some conclusions about the contents of their younger siblings' vocabularies and any changes in that content over time.

Attitudes toward words and phrases or usages of different groups offer still other possibilities. Students could compile a list of currently used hip words from their peers, compile a list of past hip words from their parents or other adults, and interview representatives of both groups on their reactions to the words. Greenman (2000), for example, has listed a number of now-dated hip expressions that make me cringe just hearing them but that I am quite sure I used rather extensively and proudly as a youngster. Students might take such a list and interview their parents and other adults to see if they used them in the past, if they now use them, and what their present response to them is. Students could ask similar questions of their peers.

Alternately, or in addition, students could collect contemporary terms from their peers, and ask their parents and other adults if they know their meanings and how they react to them. It would be interesting to compare not only the actual words used to represent various concepts but also the concepts the words represent. Which new words represent the same concepts that were important to teenagers 25 or 30 years ago? Which words represent concepts that are important to teenagers today but were less important, or even unheard of, 25 or 30 years ago? Comparing a dictionary published 20 years ago with one published more recently is another way to study changes in words and concepts.

Another possibility, this one particularly appropriate for Internet users, is for students to investigate usage variation across geographic areas. Minnesotans, for example, use *rubber binders* to hold things together. Is this use restricted to Minnesota? Wisconsin students look for a *bubbler* if they're thirsty. What do Californians, New Yorkers, or Floridians drink from? E-mail offers a convenient way to ask these and other questions about word usage.

Still another possibility is to engage students in explorations such as those suggested by Andrews in *Language Exploration and Awareness* (1998). In the following investigation, a slightly modified version of one Andrews presents, junior or senior high students explore the language of uniforms.

> Directions to Students: Prepare a collage of photographs and drawings of people dressed in formal and informal uniforms. Then be prepared to lead a class discussion of the following questions:
> 1. Why do people wear uniforms?
> 2. What happens when a person is "out of uniform" when he or she is expected to be wearing it?
> 3. How many formal and informal "uniforms" do you wear, and for what purposes or activities do you wear them?
> 4. Why are particular uniforms designed as they are? What "statement" does each of the uniforms you are considering make?
> 5. Based on your study of uniforms, how would you describe the language of uniforms? How is the language of uniforms similar to and different from the language we typically speak?

More ambitious than any of these investigations, however, and an excellent example of the sort of learning experience that investigations can provide and the quality of work students are capable of, is a project completed by Scott Rasmussen and Derek Oosterman (1999), two seniors at Minnetonka High School in Minnesota. This project, completed as part of an advanced placement psychology class, was designed to investigate procedures for teaching vocabulary. Their goal was to "determine the best means of vocabulary acquisition in high school students" (p. 1). They began with a review of the literature. Based on their reading, they then developed this set of hypotheses:

> Methods with a weightier impact on neural connections will have greater success in encoding, storage, and retrieval. Processing is theorized to be stronger when it is (1) applied continuously and frequently, (2) approached explicitly and actively, and (3) aided with creative clues incorporating several senses. (p. 1)

To investigate these hypotheses, Rasmussen and Oosterman worked with three English teachers and 12 high school classes, and arranged a number of experimental comparisons. For example, in one experiment,

Classes were presented the words in ways successively involving more and stronger sensory clues. The first class was a control, and took the test with absolutely no instruction, or with zero senses involved. The next class was presented the information visually on an overhead, but with no auditory instruction. The third class was presented the information verbally, but with no visual information. The last class learned with the aid of both the verbal sense with the overhead and the auditory sense with the researchers reading the words and definitions. (pp. 1–2)

The hypothesis investigated in this part of the study was confirmed: Incorporating more senses led to better word learning, with the four groups described above receiving scores of 42%, 77%, 74%, and 86%, respectively. Not surprisingly, other results confirmed some of their hypotheses and failed to confirm others.

The point is not so much what Rasmussen and Oosterman learned about vocabulary instruction as the extent to which the experience is likely to leave them with a heightened awareness of words. I have corresponded with one of these young researchers, Rasmussen, about his work, and he reports that he now pays more attention to words than he used to. "Before the study," he wrote, "I never gave vocabulary much thought. . . . In regular conversations and school classes now, I am increasingly cognizant of how words can influence perception and meaning." Although investigations as complex as this project are likely to be rare, almost any study in which students examine some lexical phenomena is likely to leave them more conscious of words.

TEACHING STUDENTS ABOUT WORDS

Most of the activities discussed thus far encourage students to become aware of words, manipulate them, appreciate them, and play with them in ways that do not involve explicit instruction. In this final section of the chapter, I consider some knowledge about words that teachers and teacher educators should definitely have and the possibility of explicitly instructing students on some of these. The section draws heavily on a recent chapter by Nagy and Scott (2000) in which they discuss the complexity of word knowledge and the role of metalinguistic awareness in learning words.

The Complexity of Word Knowledge

According to Nagy and Scott (2000), if we are to understand the processes underlying students' vocabulary growth—and, I would add, if we are to effectively assist that growth—we must recognize at least five aspects of the complexity of word knowledge. These five aspects are *incrementality, multidimensionality, polysemy, interrelatedness,* and *heterogeneity*. More recently, Scott and Nagy (2004) have added a sixth aspect, understanding the role of definitions, context, and word parts in vocabulary learning.

Incrementality. Word learning is incremental; that is, it proceeds in a series of steps. As Clark (1993) has pointed out, the meanings young children initially assign to words are incomplete, but over time these meanings become increasingly refined until they eventually approximate those of adults. *Dog*, for example, may at first refer to any small animal—dogs, cats, hamsters, squirrels—and only later be applied exclusively to dogs. School-age children and adults take a similar course in learning many of the words they eventually master. Dale (1965) attempted to capture this incremental nature of word learning by proposing four levels of word knowledge: (1) never having seen it before, (2) knowing there is such a word, but not knowing what it means, (3) having a vague and context-bound meaning for the word, and (4) knowing and remembering it. Dale's fourth level could be further broken down—into, for example, having a full and precise meaning versus having a general meaning, or using the word in writing versus only recognizing it when reading. However levels of word knowledge are defined, it is clear that reaching high levels is no mean task. McKeown, Beck, Omanson, and Pople (1985) found that even 40 high-quality instructional encounters with words did not bring students to a ceiling. It is also clear that high levels of word knowledge are needed to effect reading comprehension, and that only powerful instruction produces such high levels (Stahl & Fairbanks, 1986; Nagy, 1988).

Multidimensionality. The second aspect of word knowledge, its being multidimensional, is in some ways a qualification on the first. Although it is useful to think of levels of word knowledge, in actuality there is no single dimension along which differences in word knowledge can be considered. As I pointed out in Chapter 2, Calfee and Drum (1986) note that knowing a word involves "depth of meaning; precise usage; facile access . . . ; the ability to articulate one's understanding; flexibility in the application of the knowledge of the word; the appreciation of metaphor, analogy, word play; the ability to recognize a synonym, to define, to use a word expressively" (pp. 825–826). To this, I would add a central theme of this chapter, that word knowledge has both a cognitive and an affective component.

Polysemy. The third aspect of words, polysemy, refers to the fact that many words have multiple meanings. Polysemy is more frequent than it is often thought to be; a lot of words have multiple meanings, and the more frequent the word, the more likely it is to have two or more meanings. Additionally, it is worth recognizing that the multiple meanings of words range from cases in which the meanings are completely unrelated (the *bank* of a river versus the *bank* where you cash checks) to cases in which the differences are so subtle that it is difficult to decide whether or not they are indeed different meanings (*giving* Mary $10 versus *giving* Mary a kiss). Moreover, words virtually always gain some meaning from the context in which they are found, with the result that meanings are infinitely nuanced.

Interrelatedness. The fourth aspect of words to note is their interrelatedness: A learner's knowledge of one word is linked to his knowledge of other words. To use Nagy and Scott's (2000) example, "How well a person knows the meaning of *whale* depends in part on his or her understanding of *mammal*. A person who already knows the words *hot*, *cold*, and *cool* has already acquired some of the components of the word *warm*, even if the word *warm* has not yet been encountered" (p. 272).

Heterogeneity. The fifth aspect of words to be concerned with is their heterogeneity: What it means to know a word is dependent on the type of word in question. To again use Nagy and Scott's (2000) example, "knowing function words such as *the* or *if* is quite different from knowing terms such as *hypotenuse* or *ion*" (p. 273). But it is not just different words that require different sorts of knowing. Different word users require different sorts of word knowledge. As a potential purchaser of a diamond engagement ring, a young man is certainly better served if he has some knowledge of diamonds. As a seller of diamond rings and possibly a large-scale purchaser of diamonds, a jeweler needs and typically has considerably more knowledge of diamonds than his customers. And as the artisan and artist who shapes a beautiful stone from an unremarkable piece of rock, a diamond cutter must have both richer and quite different knowledge than the jeweler.

Definitions, Context, and Word Parts. This last aspect of words that Scott and Nagy (2004) consider includes topics that I have discussed in detail in Chapter 6 as part of teaching students word-learning strategies. The point that Scott and Nagy make about the need for students to understand word-learning strategies is that in addition to knowing *how to use* word-learning strategies, students need to know some things *about* word-learning strategies. Most notably, students need to understand when to use these strategies, when not to use them, and the strengths and limitations of each of them. Definitions, for example, are useful for checking on the meaning of a word you think you know or for getting some general idea of a word's meaning. They are not useful for learning rich and precise word meanings. Somewhat differently, it is useful for students to understand that many English words come from Latin and Greek roots.

The Role of Metalinguistic Awareness in Word Learning

What sorts of metalinguistic awareness of words and word learning are important to teachers and to students? The question with respect to teachers can be easily answered. Everything in this section of the chapter, everything in Nagy and Scott's (2000) chapter, and a good deal of the information contained in the references to this chapter and to Nagy and Scott's chapter is important for teachers. Understanding incrementality, multidimensionality, polysemy, interrelatedness, and heterogeneity cannot help but be valuable to you as you work with students. Additionally, Andrews's *Language Exploration and Awareness* (1998) offers a number of insights about words and about other aspects of language that teachers and teacher educators should find useful. Similarly, a recent chapter by Nagy (in press) contains an extremely convincing argument for the importance of metalinguistic awareness.

The answer with respect to students is not as easily arrived at. While some metalinguistic awareness about words and word learning can certainly be valuable to students, just what students need to learn and how they can best learn it are matters yet to be decided. One could attempt to directly teach students a body of knowledge about words much like instruction in traditional grammar was once used to teach knowledge about sentences. But I strongly suspect that such an attempt would yield poor results, and perhaps even produce the negative attitude toward words that grammar instruction often produced toward language study. Instead, it seems likely that much of this knowledge should be embedded in students' ongoing work with words and be brought to conscious attention as appropriate opportunities arise.

Here are three examples. Polysemy can be appropriately dealt with when students are being instructed in using dictionaries or when they are actually using them to look up word meanings. Certainly, one of the principles students should follow when looking up definitions is to choose the definition that fits the context in which they find the word, and this means recognizing that words have different meanings that are both shaped and revealed by context. Incrementality can be appropriately dealt with when students are learning to use context to unlock word meanings. Something that students who are learning to use context clues to identify word meanings need to recognize is that a single instance of a word in context is likely to reveal only a small increment of a word's meaning, but that each additional instance of the word in context is likely to reveal another increment. Finally, interrelatedness can be appropriately dealt with when students are learning new concepts, particularly when they are learning concepts in a relatively unfamiliar domain. Students who are studying literary elements of narratives, for example, will need to learn the meanings of *rising action, falling action,* and *plot* as part of learning the meaning of *climax;* and the context of their doing so provides an excellent opportunity for introducing the notion of the interrelatedness of words.

Additionally, students will learn a lot about words as part of engaging in many of the informal learning experiences described throughout this chapter. The adept diction that professional writers use is possible because there are so many different words available to choose from. Much word play—puns, for example—works because words have multiple meanings. And intensive instruction is necessary because word learning is an incremental process. These and other insights about words can be briefly pointed out as students are involved in these various activities.

As these considerations of teaching students about words demonstrate, some approaches to word consciousness are fairly complex and academic, and such approaches certainly have a place. Nonetheless, we need to remember that one definite purpose of word consciousness work is to foster our students' enthusiasm about words, a fact illustrated in Figure 6.2.

CONCLUDING REMARKS

The purpose of this chapter has been to define and elaborate on the concept of word consciousness, to argue for the importance of word consciousness as a deliberate goal of vocabulary instruction, and to suggest some approaches to fostering word consciousness. The student who is word conscious knows a lot of words, and he knows them well. Equally importantly, he is interested in words, and he gains enjoyment and satisfaction from using them well and from seeing or hearing them used well by others. He finds words intriguing, recognizes adroit word usage when he encounters it, uses words adroitly himself, is on the

Figure 6.2 Give Me a Big W

Words!   Words!   Words!

lookout for new and precise words, and is responsive to the nuances of word meanings. He is also cognizant of the power of words and realizes that they can be used to foster clarity and understanding or to obscure and obfuscate matters. Given the size and complexity of the task of learning tens of thousands of words, developing students' word consciousness so that they have both the will and the skill to improve their vocabularies is hugely important. However, despite the importance and complexity of the vocabulary learning task, it makes good sense to keep most efforts to foster word consciousness light and low keyed. Whenever possible, word consciousness activities should encourage a playfulness like that shown in these snippets of word play I recently came across:

> If ignorance is bliss, why aren't more people happy?
> Why is the man who invests all your money called a broker?
> When cheese gets its picture taken, what does it say?

Or like that shown by these winners of the *Washington Post's* annual contest in coming up with alternate meanings for words:

> flabbergasted—appalled over how much weight you have gained
> lymph—to walk with a lisp

CHAPTER 7

Classroom Portraits of Effective Vocabulary Instruction

Over the past 25 years, I've taught in almost every type of school—suburban, urban, and rural—and at almost every grade level—first through twelfth. And I can tell you that vocabulary is crucial in every type of school and at every grade level. Now that I'm a principal, that's one of the main messages I try to communicate to all of my teachers—"Help all kids learn the words of their language, and you'll go a long way toward helping them become skillful readers, skillful writers, and skillful communicators."

Nancy Bigelow, middle school principal

As I hope has been evident throughout this book, I am in total agreement with Nancy Bigelow. Words are tremendously important to students' success in and out of school, and we need to do everything possible to help them acquire rich and powerful vocabularies. In reading, competence in such areas as phonemic awareness, phonics, fluency, and various aspects of comprehension are also important. So too are a variety of competencies and knowledge in science, math, social studies, literature, and other areas of the curriculum. But words are vital in all these curricular areas and therefore a primary concern of all teachers.

Up to this point in the book, I have described the four-part vocabulary curriculum I am recommending in some detail. In this chapter, I paint portraits of some very skillful teachers implementing vocabulary instruction in their classrooms. More specifically, the four sections of this chapter present vignettes from a first-grade classroom, a fourth-grade classroom, an eighth-grade classroom, and several eleventh-grade classrooms.

KARREN SILL'S FIRST-GRADE CLASSROOM

It is obvious when you walk into Karren Sill's first-grade classroom that listening, speaking, reading, and writing are encouraged here. The room is rich with environmental print—labels on objects and special places, messages or special words on colorful bulletin boards—there is a well-stocked classroom library, and all around the room you find inviting places to read and write or to listen to recorded books and stories. There can be no doubt that the first graders in Karren's room are getting the message that words, those essential tools for thinking and communicating, are important here.

The variety of activities that take place in Karren's room also give testimony to the importance of words, to building students' vocabularies, to their understanding the meaning of words and recognizing these words in print. Karren believes that her first graders will benefit most from two of the four parts of the comprehensive vocabulary program—providing rich and varied language experiences and promoting word consciousness. As a result, she spends most of her time on these two. The following portrait illustrates a few of the ways Karren puts these two emphases into practice with her group of 20 five- and six-year-olds on a bright and sunny day early in the school year.

One of the first activities of the day is the morning message. The children gather on the floor around Karren, who prints a message on a large chart on an easel. First, she writes the words, "Morning News" at the top. Next, she writes "Today is Tuesday. Outside it is . . ."

Annika suggests the word *sunny*. This is a word children have chosen often before, so Karren encourages them to think of another word. Noah comes up with *sparkly* and another student *breezy*. Karren writes these words on the chart and the class talks briefly about what these words mean.

After this discussion, children give news of the world and of their neighborhoods and families. Again, Karren writes the students' statements on the chart for students to see. They read them together. Karren may stop occasionally to point out an interesting word or ask for another word that could mean the same thing. In doing this, she is both providing a meaningful language experience and promoting word consciousness.

Another activity Karren uses in her classroom is Text Talk (Beck & McKeown, 2001; McKeown & Beck, 2003). As you will recall from Chapter 3, Text Talk is an interactive book reading procedure that fosters comprehension and helps develop young children's vocabularies by focusing on sophisticated words that are likely to appear in material students will read themselves in the future. For this Text Talk activity, Karren has selected *A Spree in Paree* by Catherine Stock, a story that invites discussion and includes some rich vocabulary. She has chosen four words to focus on: *spree, chagrin, collapsed*, and the French word *baguettes*.

A Spree in Paree is the rollicking story of a hardworking French farmer, Monsieur Monmouton, who takes his animals—or rather is taken by them!—on a spree to Paris. They visit Paris's many famous sites all in one day, which completely exhausts the poor farmer. At the end of the day back at his home, Monsieur Monmouton collapses in his armchair complaining, "These holidays are too much work for me." The animals, however, are not at all tuckered out, and the barn hums with noise as they busily plan their next outing.

To begin their work with Text Talk, Karren reads this 600-word story aloud with enthusiasm and expression, without stopping for questions or discussion. Then she reads the story a second time, pausing to ask questions that require the children to describe and explain ideas. Her first question comes after reading Monsieur Monmouton's statement, "I could do with a holiday. But who would look after my animals?"

> *Karren:* What do you think Monsieur Monmouton means when he says, "I could do with a holiday"?
> *MacKensie:* He needs to have some fun.
> *Karren:* Good. Anything else?
> *Garrett:* Rest. He needs to take a day off.
> *Karren:* Good. Why do you think he needs to have fun and to rest?
> *Sarai:* He works too hard . . . all those animals to take care of.
> *Karren:* Good thinking.

Karren reads some more of the story, stopping occasionally to ask questions like these: Why do you think the geese waddled down to the river Seine? . . . the goats were interested in the gardens at Luxembourg? . . . the pigeons wanted to check out the Eiffel Tower? . . . the pigs were interested in dinner at a fancy restaurant?

At the conclusion of her second reading of the story, Karren asks, "What did Monsieur Monmouton think of the holiday in Paris? Why do you think so? What did the animals think of their holiday? Why do you think so?"

Next, Karren concentrates on the vocabulary she has preselected. Here is the procedure she used for the word *spree*.

1. Describes how the word is used in the story

   Karren: A Spree in Paree. I like that rhyming title. And I like the word *spree*. It's a great word for the title of this story. Paree is how Paris is pronounced in French. Can you say "spree in Paree"? (The children repeat "spree in Paree.")

2. Explains the word's meaning and a situation in which it might be used

   Karren: A spree is a fun, lively outing . . . like Monsieur Monmouton and his animals had in Paree! They went into a city with lots of interesting things to see and do and they did them. They had a great time. Oui, Oui! (Pronounced we, we.) Oui, oui means "yes, yes" in French. Can you say "Oui, Oui?" (Children repeat "Oui, Oui!")

3. Has the children say the word

   Karren: Say the word with me, *spree*. (Children say *spree*.) Say it again. (Children say *spree*.) Oui, oui a spree in Paree!

4. Gives examples of the word in contexts other than the story

   Karren: My mother and I sometimes go on a shopping spree. We go from store to store, looking at all the things for sale, and sometimes buying things. We always have a fun, lively time. You might go on a spree to Disneyworld or to the zoo or to a city like New York where there are lots of interesting things to see, like the Statue of Liberty and the Empire State Building.

5. Has children make judgments about the word

   Karren: Which place could you go on a spree? To the doctor's office or to an amusement park?

6. Has children give examples and provides feedback

   Karren: Think of some place you might go on a spree. Start your sentence with "I could go on a spree to . . . ."

   Blake: I could go on a spree to the movies.

   Karren: Yes, movies can be fun to go to . . . at least some movies. But when I go to the movies, it's not really all that lively. I mean, I just sit there and watch the screen. How might the movies be a spree, a fun, lively outing?

   Annabel: If Monsieur Monmouton were there with all his animals!!

   Karren: That *would* be lively, and noisy, and a mess, and . . .

   Mike: and probably no one would watch the movie and they'd have to turn it off.

   Karren: I don't think most people find the movies the best place to have a spree. What other places might we go on a spree?

   Cooper: I could go on a spree to the beach.

Karren: Yes, especially if you brought friends along, food to eat, a radio, and a beach ball and other things to play with! That would be a lively, fun time! A spree!
7. Reinforces the pronunciation and meaning of the word
   Karren: What's the word that means a fun, lively outing?
   Children: A spree!

Karren's presentation of the word *spree* took somewhat longer than she anticipated, so she changed her plans a bit and decided to introduce only one more word instead of three. She chose *collapsed* as the second word because it fit into the theme of the story and the discussion of the word *spree*: The *spree* to Paree was so lively, and fun (and exhausting) that Monsieur Monmouton *collapsed* in his armchair at the end of the outing.

As a follow-up to this Text Talk activity, Karren added the focus words from the story—*spree* and *collapsed*—to a bulletin board of special words. During center time, children made up picture stories using the words taught that day and some words that they had previously learned.

This of course is only one morning in Karren's class. Other days will be different. But on all days Karren will do at least some work with words, work designed to help her first graders on the long road to acquiring full and rich vocabularies.

GARY SUTTON'S FOURTH-GRADE ROOM

Gary Sutton teaches fourth grade in a suburban school in California. His students represent all levels of ability and a number of different ethnic and racial backgrounds, but they have one thing in common. They have an appreciation for words. Why? Because Gary, a writer and avid reader, has instilled his enthusiasm for words in his students.

Like Karren Sill's first-grade classroom, Gary's room attests to his own and his students' interest in words—a library stocked with books and periodicals representing every genre and ranging in readability from easy-to-read nonfiction books such as Gail Gibbons's *Grizzly Bears* to challenging novels such as John Steinbeck's *The Pearl*, and even Harper Lee's *To Kill a Mockingbird*. The classroom also has a word wall containing words that students have been taught and are encouraged to use in their own writing; cozy places with comfortable chairs for reading; special writing centers with writing tools, including dictionaries and thesauri, computers, printers, and paper; and a game center that includes vocabulary games such as *Scrabble*, *Pictionary*, and *Balderdash*.

Across the fourth-grade curriculum—social studies, math, science, art, music, and language arts—Gary incorporates all four parts of the vocabulary program suggested in this book: providing rich and varied languages experiences, teaching individual words, teaching word-learning strategies, and fostering word consciousness are woven into the curriculum. Gary knows that the more he can give students the tools they need to unlock the meaning that language offers, the more equipped they will be for success in the classroom and out.

Virtually every day is infused with activities that stress the importance, the usefulness, and the pleasure of words. To provide a rich language experience and at the same time promote word consciousness, beginning the very first day of school, Gary reads aloud to his students—novels and stories of literary quality and high reader appeal, such as *Holes* by Louis Sachar and *Crispin* by Avi, or nonfiction texts that relate to some part of the curriculum, perhaps Linda Lowery's *One More Valley, One More Hill*, a biography of black pioneer Aunt Clara Brown, or a well-written and enticing informational book such as Jane Goodall's *The Chimpanzees I Love: Saving Their World and Ours*.

In addition to expanding students' knowledge of various concepts, Gary knows reading aloud exposes his students to words they might not hear in conversation or on television. Occasionally while reading, he pauses to admire an author's word choice or point out a word that relates to something students have been focusing on. For example, the class has been working on using strong verbs in their writing, so while reading aloud Avi's *True Confessions of Charlotte Doyle*, Gary stops to point out *pocketed* and *lumbered* in the sentence, "The money *pocketed*, the man *lumbered* over to my trunk, swung it to his shoulder with astonishing ease—considering the trunk's weight and size—and said, 'Lead on.'"

"Imagine," Gary says, "the same sentence with the more common, but duller verbs *taken* instead of *pocketed* and *walked* instead of *lumbered*. "The money *taken*, the man *walked* over to my trunk, swung it to his shoulder with astonishing ease—considering the trunk's weight and size—and said, 'Lead on.'"

Gary uses this opportunity to talk about the images that *pocketed* and *lumbered* create in the reader's mind that *taken* and *walked* could not. He asks some volunteers to dramatize these words and other volunteers to write the words on tagboard strips to add to their word wall. Now the students have both a visual image of the meaning of each word and its representation in writing.

To get a sense of his students' general word knowledge, during the first weeks of the school year and occasionally throughout the year, Gary uses two kinds of assessments: informal tests and oral spot checks. The informal tests, which Gary creates himself, contain words from the various texts students will be reading. Before giving these tests, he shares his reason for using them. "These are not tests you'll be graded on," Gary tells his fourth graders. "They're to help me understand what words you know and what ones you don't know. This information will guide me in choosing which words to help you learn."

The other technique Gary occasionally uses to assess his students' word knowledge is writing potentially difficult words on the board and asking students which ones they don't know. For example, before students embark on a unit of study of the California missions, he writes these words on the board—*mission, adobe, Indian, Catholic, religious, missionary, Spanish, tradition, courtyard, protection*—and asks for a show of hands as he points to each word, recording the number of students who raise their hands for each. By using these two sorts of tests to discover words his students do and don't know, Gary both avoids the wasted effort of teaching students words they already know and makes it more likely that he will teach the crucial vocabulary they do not know.

Throughout the year, before students read on their own, for whatever subject or purpose, Gary usually teaches a few of the words that might prove stumbling blocks. If a word is in students' oral but not reading vocabularies, the task is fairly simple. In teaching *protection*, for example, Gary writes *protection* on the board, pronounces it, and has students say it. He then briefly defines it. If a word is new but represents an available concept, such as *tradition* might, he may use something like the Context-Relationship Procedure, which is described in Chapter 4. And if the word represents a somewhat familiar concept that needs fleshing out, as *missionary* might, he may use Semantic Mapping, another procedure described in Chapter 4.

In addition to teaching individual words, Gary incorporates work on word-learning strategies such as using context cues, word parts, and the dictionary to unlock the meaning of unknown words in the class's curriculum studies. For example, during the unit on the California missions, Gary notices that prefixes are beginning to appear in the reading students are doing and decides to present some initial instruction on using prefixes to unlock the meanings of unknown words. In doing so, he follows the procedures described in Chapter 5, teaching students a powerful procedure they can use to unlock the meanings of unknown words and the prefixes *un-*, *re-*, and *in-* over a 5-day period.

In the weeks following that initial instruction, the prefixes *un-*, *re-*, and *in-* are spotlighted in classroom and homework activities. Students collect words that contain the prefixes wherever they find them and construct a bulletin board on which lists of *un-*, *re-*, and *in-* words grow daily. Every other day or so, Gary challenges a pair of students to find the "biggest, baddest" *un-*, *re-*, and *in-* words they can and bring them to class. The next day, the pair shares their words, and explain how they used the meaning of the prefixes and the English root word to figure out the words' meanings. From time to time, Gary also asks students to identify words beginning with *un*, *re*, and *in* in which these elements are not prefixes, and some of these nonexamples are added to the bulletin board.

Over the course of the year, Gary may teach several more prefixes using this same procedure. He will also review the strategy of using context clues, which was taught in the third grade, and he will do some work with the dictionary, a tool students will learn more about in the fifth grade. As part of their dictionary work, Gary has students develop their own dictionaries—specialized dictionaries comprised of words from units they have studied.

Gary also reinforces vocabulary growth with games—fun activities using the words they've been learning in class. For one such activity, the Vocab Squad—a team of students that changes monthly—identifies challenging and interesting words from recent readings or discussions and writes the words on white note cards and their definitions on blue note cards. To play, the two sets of cards are shuffled, and each student not on the Vocab Squad is given two cards—a white card with a word and a blue card with a definition. These cards are placed face up on students' desks. The first player to have a turn reads her definition card aloud saying, for example, "who has 'the handing down of beliefs, opinions, customs, stories, etc. from parents to children?'" The student who has the word that matches the definition says, "I have *tradition*." That student then turns the white card with the vocabulary word face down, reads her blue card with a definition and asks, for example, "Who has 'brick made of clay and straw that is dried in the sun?'" The student with *adobe* responds, and the game continues until everyone has a turn.

As you can see from this brief classroom portrait, all four components of the comprehensive vocabulary program described in this book—providing rich and varied languages experiences, teaching individual words and word-learning strategies, and promoting word consciousness—have an important place in Gary Sutton's fourth-grade class. And because vocabulary is given such emphasis, these fourth graders are on their way to acquiring the sorts of vocabularies that will serve them well—not only in the fourth grade, but in the fifth grade, middle school, high school, and beyond.

DARCY ANDREWS'S MIDDLE SCHOOL CLASSROOM

When Darcy Andrews moved from teaching in an affluent suburban school to an urban school, one of the many differences she noticed was the disparity in the academic vocabularies of her suburban and urban students. Darcy taught eighth-grade English, and vocabulary was something she considered crucially important. The majority of her urban students, even the brightest and most motivated, fell short of the command of the language demonstrated by many of her suburban students. Not that the urban students didn't have substantial vocabularies—they knew a lot of words—but they didn't know nearly as many as the suburban students, and the words they knew weren't the ones that would serve them best in school and in many pursuits outside of school. And it wasn't just the English learners who lagged behind. Only a small percentage of students in Darcy's classes possessed vocabularies comparable to those of her former students. She had read about such disparities in her university courses, but now she was seeing them firsthand.

Because Darcy knew this sort of disparity put her urban students at a disadvantage with their suburban peers, she was determined to help close the gap. She wanted her urban students to have all the advantages that word knowledge gives a person, the thinking and communicative power that words can provide, and she was determined to do what she could to motivate students to increase their vocabularies and expand their knowledge of words and what words can do. A tall order, perhaps, but Darcy was motivated. She knew that a vocabulary deficit was a key factor underlying school failure for many disadvantaged students, and she wanted these students to succeed in school and in life.

Darcy's district had adopted a literature series for Grades 7–9, and it included a vocabulary strand. Most of the series's vocabulary instruction was delivered on the computer, and it focused on two of the four elements recommended in this book: teaching individual words and teaching word-learning strategies. Darcy took advantage of the prepared materials and the computer delivery, which her students enjoyed, and reinforced these two important elements whenever appropriate.

However, Darcy's vocabulary program didn't end there. Since English classes are involved in reading, writing, listening, and speaking, a significant portion of her class time was devoted to the other two parts of a comprehensive vocabulary program: providing rich and varied languages experiences and promoting word consciousness. Darcy emphasized these for two important reasons: (1) because she knew it was critical for her students to be immersed in the kind of language experiences that kindled an appreciation for words, and (2) because they fit well with her personal philosophy about the critical importance of motivation. One of Darcy's strongest and most enduring beliefs as a teacher was that you have to get kids interested in and excited about a topic before much learning will take place.

So, Darcy knew where she had to start—with the kids themselves. She needed to find out what they knew and what they were interested in. On Friday of the first week of school, she had them write self-portraits that told about their interests, their heroes, and their aspirations. They could use any writing form they wanted—a letter to a pen pal, a poem or rap song, or a brief essay—forms that Darcy briefly explained and modeled.

Darcy used these self-portraits to learn not only about the interests and yearnings of her students, but also about their expressive vocabularies. This information then became the basis for the listening, reading, word learning, discussion, and writing experiences she would provide. It also informed the sorts of books, magazines, and other materials— such as word-play books, song sheets, books of rap and other types of poetry—she would make available in her classroom library and the visual displays she would create to promote words.

The first of these visual displays appeared on Monday of the second week of school. Covering one entire wall, Darcy had created a bulletin board titled "Word Power" featuring many of the words students had used in their self-portraits, plus pictures of the students' heroes clipped from magazines and other sources. The first vocabulary lesson these eighth graders received that year involved these words, their own words—their meanings, their sounds, the contexts in which students had used them, and why they were examples of good word choices, of word power. The lesson also included both Darcy and students suggesting words that might be used in place of the highlighted words and ended with Darcy's admission that she was a "word nut," and that by the end of the year she hoped they would be too.

What Darcy didn't tell her students was that the words she would be stealthfully (and at times not so stealthfully) teaching them, the words that they would be adding to their listening and speaking vocabularies, were very carefully selected. These were words that played important roles in the materials students were reading that year, and words that her students were likely to encounter later in their school experiences; challenging words that were used across domains—English, history, science; words that were a bit of a stretch for these students. And

Darcy wanted to stretch her students, narrow that gap between them and their more advantaged counterparts in the suburbs, and give them tools for learning, thinking, and communicating.

During the second week, too, Darcy began what would be standard fare in all her classes: reading quality literature aloud—a book, story, essay, nonfiction piece, or a poem—that was accessible and interesting to students but a bit challenging in the words it included. The selections she chose offered opportunities to introduce students to new words and allow them to experience the rich, precise, interesting, and inventive use of words. Each day, Darcy read for 5 minutes; then students selected a mutually agreed-upon word from the selection to add to the Word Power bulletin board and include in their personal Word Power books.

In addition to providing opportunities for students to grow in their appreciation of the power of words, gain an understanding of why certain words are used instead of others, and add important, colorful, and useful words to their listening and reading vocabularies, Darcy had another goal. She wanted students to actively use the words they were learning in their speech and writing.

One method Darcy used to accomplish this goal was the Word Power Miniscript. For this activity, students wrote and performed 3- to 5-minute miniscripts using the words they'd added to the Word Power bulletin board that week and had recorded in their personal Word Power books. Miniscripts were assigned as homework and performed every other Friday—Word Power Friday. The students worked in groups of two to five to collaboratively write and perform their scripts on Word Power Fridays. The goal was to use at least five of the Word Power words in the script at least once. Before writing their scripts, the students had worked with these words in different ways—looking up definitions, creating alternate definitions, seeing the words in various contexts, investigating relationships between these words and others with similar but subtly different meanings, and generally engaging in the sorts of Rich Instruction activities described in Chapter 4—so they had a good grasp of the words.

Darcy encouraged students to be as creative as they liked. The only rule was that no offensive language or subject matter could be used. These were G-rated scripts. The performances took about 30 minutes of class time every other Friday.

The class developed the first few miniscripts as whole-class writing activities, and volunteers took turns performing the parts. After several performances, Darcy held a discussion on what worked and what could be done to improve the scripts and their performances. After this, the miniscripts were group projects.

Here is a sample miniscript using the words *prevail, adorn, scorn, shabby, confidant,* all of which were taken from *Free to Dream: The Making of a Poet* by Audrey Osofsky, a biography of Langston Hughes that Darcy had read aloud from that week.

Scene: A diner

Big Man (walking into diner and spying a man dining alone in a
   booth): Hey, man. You lookin' *shabby*. No smile to *adorn*
   your face? Z'up bro?

Little Man (playing with his food): Don't *scorn* me, man.

(Waitress whispers in Little Man's ear)

Big Man: Who's she? Your *confidant?*

Little man: (jumps up) I will *prevail!*

Big Man (looking at waitress): What did you put in his food?

Waitress: You're accusing me because this man is a little excited
   about his life? You don't want your friend to *prevail*, to
   succeed?

Big Man (looking guilty): Come on, bro'. *Adorn* yourself with a
   smile. Let's go *prevail* together!

(Big Man and Little Man walk out of the diner together.)

After several weeks of writing and performing the Word Power miniscripts, the students asked Darcy if they could add something to Word Power Fridays—competition. They wanted to model Word Power Friday and the miniscripts after the TV series *Last Comic Standing* and call it "Last Script Standing." The class would vote on their favorite script each Friday, and at the end of the year they'd have a showdown of all the winning scripts. Darcy agreed with their plan, as long as everyone was happy with the idea and respectful and kind toward each other's work. The competition factor really raised the stakes in terms of interest, involvement, and ownership. As a result, the scripts improved each week, and these eighth graders' use, knowledge, and appreciation of words improved right along with them.

By the end of the year, Darcy knew her students had markedly increased their listening, reading, speaking, and writing vocabularies, maybe not to equal those of their suburban peers, but the gap had definitely been narrowed. And, perhaps even more important, her students had gained a genuine appreciation for words and had acquired valuable word-learning tools that would serve them well in the years ahead.

THREE HIGH SCHOOL TEACHERS AND THEIR CLASSES

In high school, of course, students don't have just one or two teachers, they have five or six of them, and each teacher sees them for an hour or less a day. This means that if students are going to get a lot of help in building their vocabularies, they need to get it from more than one teacher, from more than the English teacher. In this section, I describe some of the vocabulary activities provided by three eleventh-grade teachers—an English teacher, a social studies teacher, and a science teacher.

Allen Halstad, Stacy Post, and Robert Rivera all began as first-year teachers at Richfield High School 5 years ago—Allen in English, Stacy in social studies, and Robert in science. Since they were about the same age and faced with similar demands and challenges, they rapidly became friends and supporters of each others' efforts, and those relationships grew and strengthened over the 5 years. The three do not have offices together and only share the same prep period from time to time, but one effort on which they have managed to collaborate some is vocabulary instruction. As an English teacher, Allen had always had a strong interest in vocabulary, and several years ago he took a university course that particularly emphasized the potential of teaching vocabulary across the curriculum. Allen thought the suggestions for cross-curricular cooperation in vocabulary instruction really sound and talked up the idea with his two colleagues, and their collaboration began. It's not an elaborate plan, and as an English teacher Allen puts more emphasis on vocabulary than Stacy or Robert. But both Stacy and Robert are convinced of the importance of words in their subjects, and both make substantial contributions to their students' vocabulary growth. Here is the arrangement they came up with.

Allen takes responsibility for making suggestions to the other two, and as I just noted, spends more time on vocabulary than the others. If you observed Allen's classes over a period of weeks, you would see some attention to all four parts of a comprehensive program—rich and varied language experiences (lots of reading, writing, and discussion), teaching individual words (usually in conjunction with something students are reading in common, but occasionally as part of a writing activity in which certain words are likely to be useful), teaching word-learning strategies (by the eleventh grade almost all students have learned to use context, word parts, and the dictionary, but Allen often takes a minute to remind students of these strategies and prompt them to use them where appropriate), and promoting word consciousness (a day seldom goes by that Allen doesn't do something to interest students in words).

If you observed Stacy's and Robert's classes over the same period of time, you almost certainly would not see all four parts of a comprehensive program, but you would see some vocabulary instruction. In her social studies classes, Stacy makes particular use of Semantic Mapping and Semantic Feature Analysis. She believes that each of these activities provides students with the active learning experiences they need to master the many history concepts that are at the center of the discipline. Stacy's classes also do a lot of reading, not just for the sake of learning words, of course, but learning words is certainly one of the benefits. In his sciences classes, Robert takes a different slant. Prefixes and roots, which of course are extremely prevalent in science terminology and helpful in both learning and remembering terms, are the focus of the vocabulary work in Robert's classes. The following portraits give you a brief look into each classroom.

An American Literature Class

Both of Allen Halstad's American literature classes—his first-period class of average and below-average students, and his second-period honors class—read Faulkner's short story, "A Rose for Emily." For both classes, Allen focused on the same half dozen words from the story—*dignity, monument, imperviousness, haughty, tranquil, perverse*—words that Faulkner uses to describe the main character, Miss Emily.

Allen began his first-period-class vocabulary work with the Concept-Relationship Procedure, a procedure with which his students were familiar. As described in Chapter 4, this procedure presents a target word three or four times in a brief paragraph, which is followed by a multiple-choice item designed to check students' understanding of the word. Before his students began working independently on the procedure, he introduced the Faulkner story by giving students some background on the southern setting and culture of the town in "A Rose for Emily" and by encouraging students to think of similarities to towns they had lived in and the values and mind-set of the people there. Then he asked them to come up with words that describe any unusual or interesting people from these towns and wrote these words on the board.

Next, he told students, "Faulkner uses lots of colorful words in his stories. I chose six of those for us to take a closer look at. The ones I've chosen are those Faulkner uses to describe the main character, Miss Emily." Allen then used a transparency to walk students through the Concept-Relationship Procedure for the word *dignity*, calling on volunteers to read the sentences in the paragraph and then having students consider the multiple-choice items and choose the correct response.

It was beneath Miss Emily's *dignity* to accept any sort of charity. Her *dignity* caused her to hold her head high and to expect people to treat her with respect. A person with *dignity* behaves in a way that shows respect for herself and for others.

    Dignity means

    _____ A. poise and self-respect

    _____ B. odor and texture

    _____ C. lack of understanding

After this, Allen wrote the remaining five target words—*monument, imperviousness, haughty, tranquil, perverse*—on the board, pronounced them, and gave students a Context-Relationship worksheet he had created. Students had 10 minutes to read the five paragraphs silently and choose the best definition for each word. After students finished with the worksheet, they reviewed it as a class, making sure everyone understood the meaning of the words.

Allen then asked students to think about people they knew who could be described with these words. Who do they know who might be described as a *monument*? Why? Do they know anyone who is *haughty*? What shows *haughtiness* in a person? Do they know anyone who illustrates *imperviousness*? What might a person say or do to show he or she is *impervious*?

After the discussion, Allen had students write a paragraph using as many of the target words as possible to describe either a fictitious character or someone they knew from real life.

For his honors class, Allen had a different approach with these words. After briefly introducing the story in much the same way as he did for his first-period class, Allen had students work in groups of six to develop their own Context-Relationship items. Each person in the group wrote a context-rich paragraph for one of the target words followed by a three-item multiple-choice quiz on that word. The group members then read each other's paragraphs and took the quiz, giving each other feedback on the quality of the paragraph and quiz items. When they had completed the assignment, each group shared its best paragraph with the class, and the class agreed on the best of the best paragraphs for each word. Then, with a little encouragement from Allen, a student volunteered to put these best Context-Relationship items on an electronic file for Allen to perhaps use in a future class.

The next day Allen had students talk about the kind of person *dignity, monument, imperviousness, haughty, tranquil*, and *perverse* brought to mind. Then he asked them to think about words that suggested the opposite of each of the target words and wrote those words on the board. After the list of opposites was complete, he asked students what sorts of people those words—the opposites—brought to mind? Students then wrote a character sketch using either the target words or their opposites.

The vocabulary activities Allen provided for both his classes—the Context-Relationship Procedure, discussion, and using the words in writing—provided students with many opportunities to learn the meanings of these words before meeting them in the Faulkner story and to incorporate them into their vocabularies. Of course, throughout the year, Allen engaged students in many other types of vocabulary experiences.

A History Class

Stacy Post's second-period America history class, the most heterogeneous class she had worked with in her 5 years of teaching, had been studying types of government with what appeared to be good comprehension. But after several quizzes, Stacy realized that some of the students did not really understand some of the major concepts they were studying. She decided that some additional study was needed, and she chose Semantic Mapping and Semantic Feature Analysis as appropriate for this further study.

She began with a brief review of the four types of government the students had been studying: dictatorship, direct democracy, representative democracy, and oligarchy. Next, as a whole class they developed a semantic map for each term, beginning with *dictatorship*, which Stacy wrote on the board. Students suggested terms from their reading that related to this type of government. The initial semantic map on *dictatorship* looked like that in Figure 7.1.

Figure 7.1. Initial Semantic Map for *Dictatorship*

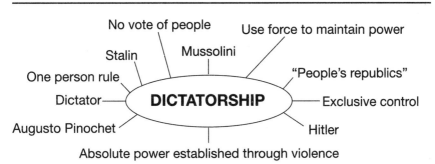

After developing this initial map on *dictatorship*, students worked in groups to refine it, grouping the terms in categories such as rulers and political leaders, attributes, and countries (see Figure 7.2).

Students then developed and refined maps on *direct democracy, representative democracy,* and *oligarchy*. Once these semantic maps were completed, Stacy had the students pair up to complete a Semantic Feature Analysis grid on the four types of governments (Figure 7.3).

These two types of activities—Semantic Mapping and Semantic Feature Analysis—helped Stacy's students refine and expand their schema for these complex concepts. Moreover, they did so in a way that let the more knowledgeable students use their knowledge and still gave all students opportunities to engage in the sorts of active processing that lead to lasting learning.

A Chemistry Class

Most of the students in Robert Rivera's sixth-period AP chemistry class will be going on to 4-year colleges, and many of them will be in the sciences, premed, prelaw, or some other field where words that make use of Latin and Greek roots and prefixes are frequently encountered. He therefore begins the year by putting a list of frequently used roots and prefixes and words that employ them on the bulletin board and

Figure 7.2. Revised Semantic Map for *Dictatorship*

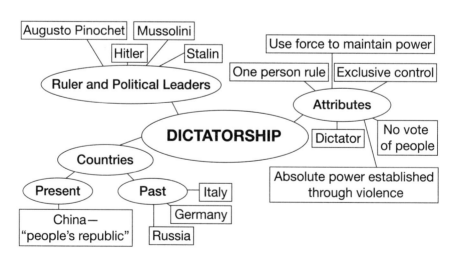

Figure 7.3. Semantic Factors Analysis Grid for *Four Types of Government*

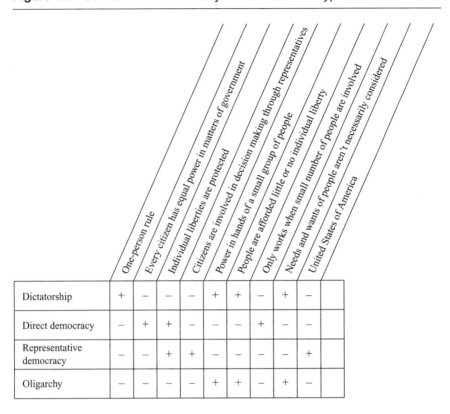

	One-person rule	Every citizen has equal power in matters of government	Individual liberties are protected	Citizens are involved in decision making through representatives	Power in hands of a small group of people	People are afforded little or no individual liberty	Only works when small number of people are involved	Needs and wants of people aren't necessarily considered	United States of America	
Dictatorship	+	−	−	−	+	+	−	+	−	
Direct democracy	−	+	+	−	−	−	+	−	−	
Representative democracy	−	−	+	+	−	−	−	−	+	
Oligarchy	−	−	−	−	+	+	−	+	−	

challenges students to bring in so many examples that they literally fill the board and have to start a new one.

These are the rules for the challenge:

- One prefix or root and related science terms can be submitted each week.
- The order in which students can submit items is determined in a random drawing.
- A student receives 20 points for her prefix or root, 2 points for each related science term she brings in, and 1 point for each additional related science term other students volunteer during class.
- Mr. Rivera is the final and uncontested judge of whether or not the terms supplied are valid science terms.

- Although the individual student with the most points at the end of the challenge in some sense "wins," the real winners are all of the students in the class because they learn a lot of roots and prefixes and a lot of science words.

During the third week of the challenge, Natasha brings in the prefix *micro-* meaning "small or minute" and a photocopied sheet of 38 science terms that use the prefix. Mr. Ramirez quickly realizes he doesn't have time to judge the validity of 38 terms and therefore assigns his students to judge them, two terms for some students and one for the others. Students take a couple of minutes to check the terms in the dictionary, a few terms are challenged and the challenges adjudicated, students contribute another six terms, and Natasha is awarded a total of 98 points. She will not be easy to beat. Of course, students will not learn all of the terms contributed, but they will learn some of them, they'll remember the meaning of *micro-* and be on the lookout for it in additional words, and they will have been reminded of the power of roots and prefixes.

CONCLUDING REMARKS

As Karen Sill, Gary Sutton, Darcy Andrews, Allen Halstad, Stacy Post, and Robert Rivera richly demonstrate, the four-part vocabulary program I describe in this book will be played out in various ways in different classrooms and at different grade levels. It will undoubtedly be played out in still other ways in other classrooms. That of course is as it should be. No single program is appropriate for all students and teachers. Nevertheless, as you decide just which parts of the program to keep and make your own, I hope you will remember several facts. Vocabulary is tremendously important in school and in the world outside of school. The vocabulary learning task that average students face is huge, and that faced by linguistically disadvantaged students and many English learners is still larger. Mastering English vocabulary is a task students begin long before entering kindergarten and something they will continue into college and perhaps beyond. Only a rich, well-planned, multifaceted, and long-term program can be a truly significant factor helping students achieve this task. The four-part plan I have described—providing rich and varied language experiences, teaching individual words, teaching word-learning strategies, and fostering word consciousness—is my very best effort at describing such a program. I hope you will consider this plan carefully as you plan your own rich and multifaceted program.

In concluding this chapter and the book as a whole, I would like to quote from a class handout distributed at the beginning of each semester by Garrard Beck, a former teacher at Washburn High School in Minneapolis. For 18 years, from 1962 when he began the course until 1980 when he retired, Mr. Beck taught a one-semester course titled Word Study. Originating as a substitute for senior English, a required course for seniors who were not taking any other English courses, Word Study became an elective and grew from a single section to five sections. It also grew into both a major part of Mr. Beck's life and an institution at the school. If each of us can develop the love and respect for words shown by Mr. Beck and articulate and communicate that love and respect to our students as he did to his, we will be well on our way to providing them with the sort of vocabulary instruction they need and deserve.

As a firm believer in the credo that one lives in his head or not at all, I view a knowledge of words as a means to this end and as a *sine qua non* of life. Every word you know is a window upon the world, and the desideratum of the struggle is to emerge from one's cellular self into a mansion of many rooms and many windows. Words are labels for the things we see and the things we feel. Without such labels we are lost, or at least confused. A certain, that is, an assured knowledge of words gives us at least a fighting chance to bring some semblance of order to the ineluctable insinuation of chaos. It might be perversely stated that man's claim to fame is his extensive and complex utilization of his thumb and his tongue, by which he has removed himself by an uncomfortable and questionable distance from his Darwinian cousins. How many of us have stood in front of the cages of chimps and gorillas, and felt uneasy about the chasm and the kinship that lay between us? And how often has the same feeling arisen when there are no bars between us, when the superficial appearances are identical or nearly so? Words make the difference: which words we use, how we understand them, and how we intend them to be understood. This—and only this—rationale and device will, in time, obtain for us the elusive genius which we insistently call humanity. A multitude of animals are more beautiful than we are, stronger, shrewder, kinder, longer lived, less troubled. Our unique distinction has yet to be claimed, but when it is, it will be essentially verbal. That is to say, the way out of the jungle is via a reasonable harmony between the word and the reality it identifies. (Garrard Beck, a master teacher who valued words and taught his students to similarly value them)

Children's and Adolescent Literature Cited

Avi. (1990). *True confessions of Charlotte Doyle.* New York: Orchard.

Avi. (2002). *Crispin: the cross of lead.* New York: Hyperion.

Babbit, N. (1975). *Tuck everlasting.* New York: Farrar, Straus and Giroux.

Base, G. (1986). *Anamalia.* New York: Harry N. Abrams.

Birdwell, N. (1977). *Clifford at the circus.* New York: Scholastic.

Clements, A. (1997). *Double trouble in Walla Walla.* Brookfield, CT: Millbrook Press.

Creech, S. (1994). *Walk two moons.* New York: Harper Collins.

Faulkner, W. F. (1995). A rose for Emily. In E. McDonald (Ed.), *Collected stories of William Faulkner.* New York: Random House. (Original work published 1930)

Freeman, D. (1978). *A pocket for Corduroy.* New York: Viking Press.

Gibbons, G. (2003). *Grizzly bears.* New York: Holiday House.

Gillman, P. (1997). *Jillian Jiggs.* New York: Scholastic.

Goodall, J. (2001). *The chimpanzees I love: Saving their world and ours.* New York: Scholastic.

Gwynne, F. (1970). *The king who rained.* New York: Simon & Schuster.

Hoffman, M. (1986). *Animals in the wild.* Milwaukee: Raintree Children's Press.

Juster, N. (1996). *The phantom tollbooth.* New York: Random House.

Keats, E. J. (1996). *The snowy day.* New York: Viking Press.

Khalsa, D. K. (1989). *Julian.* Montreal: Tundra Books.

Lee, H. (1995). *To kill a mockingbird.* New York: HarperCollins. (Original work published 1960)

Lionni, L. (1986). *It's mine!* New York: Knopf.

Lionni. L. (1969). *Alexander and the windup mouse.* New York: Scholastic.

Lowery, L. (2002). *One more valley, one more hill.* New York: Random House.

McClellan, S. S. (2000). *The chicken cat.* Marham, Ontario: Fitzhenry & Whitside.

Murphy, J. (1984). *What next, baby bear!* New York: Dial Books for Young Readers.

Osofsky, A. (1996). *Free to Dream: The making of a poet: Langston Hughes.* New York: Lothrop, Lee, & Shephard.

Sachar, L. (1998). *Holes*. New York: Farrar, Straus, Giroux.

Schertle, A. (1995). *Down the road.* San Diego: Brownder Press.

Steinbeck, J. (2002). *The pearl.* New York: Penguin Books. (Original work published 1947)

Stock, C. (2004). *A spree in Paree.* New York: Holiday House.

Vorst, J. (1994). *The alphabet from Z to A (with much confusion on the way).* New York: Macmillan.

References

Alvermann, D. E. (2000). Classroom talk about text: Is it dear, cheap, or a bargain at any price? In B. M. Taylor, M. F. Graves, & P. van den Broek (Eds.), *Reading for meaning: Fostering comprehension in the middle grades* (pp. 136–151). New York: Teachers College Press.

Anders, P. L., Bos, C. S., & Filip, D. (1984). The effect of semantic feature analysis on learning disabled students. In J. A. Niles & L. A. Harris (Eds.), *Yearbook of the National Reading Conference: Vol. 33. Changing perspectives in research on reading/language processing and instruction* (pp. 162–166). Rochester, NY: National Reading Conference.

Anderson, R. C. (1996). Research foundations to support wide reading. In V. Greaney (Ed.), *Promoting reading in developing countries* (pp. 55–77). Newark, DE: International Reading Association.

Anderson, R. C., & Nagy, W. E. (1992, Winter). The vocabulary conundrum. *American Educator, 16*(4), 14–18, 44–47.

Anderson, R. C., Wilson, P. T, & Fielding, L. G. (1988). Growth in reading and how children spend their time outside of school. *Reading Research Quarterly, 23,* 285–303.

Andrews, L. (1998). *Language exploration and awareness: A resource book for teachers* (2nd ed.). Mahwah, NJ: Erlbaum.

Anglin, J. M. (1993). Vocabulary development: A morphological analysis. *Monographs of the Society for Research in Child Development, 58*(10, Serial No. 238).

Arnold, D. H., Lonigan, C. J., Whitehurst, G. J., & Epstein, J. N. (1994). Accelerating language development through picture book reading: Replication and extension to a videotape training format. *Journal of Educational Psychology, 86,* 235–243.

Baumann, J. F., Edwards, E. C., Boland E., Olejnik, S., & Kame'enui, E. J. (2003). Vocabulary tricks: Effects of instruction in morphology and context on fifth-grade students' ability to derive and infer word meaning. *American Educational Research Journal, 40,* 447–494.

Baumann, J. F., Edwards, E. C., Font, G., Tereshinski, C. A., Kame'enui, E. J., & Olejnik, S. (2002). Teaching morphemic and contextual analysis to fifth-grade students. *Reading Research Quarterly, 37,* 150–176.

Baumann, J. F., Font, G., Edwards, E. C., & Boland, E. (2005). Strategies for teaching middle-grade students to use word-part and context clues to expand reading vocabulary. In E. Hiebert & M. L. Kamil (Eds.), *Teaching and learning vocabulary: Bringing research to practice* (pp. 179–205). Mahwah, NJ: Erlbaum.

Baumann, J. F., Kame'enui, E. J., & Ash, G. E. (2003). Research on vocabulary instructing: Voltaire redux. In J. Flood, D. Lapp, J. R. Squire, & J. M. Jensen (Eds.), *Handbook on research on teaching the English language arts* (2nd ed., pp. 752–785). Mahwah, NJ: Erlbaum.

Beck, I. L., McCaslin, E. S., & McKeown, M. G. (1980). *The rationale and design of a program to teach vocabulary to fourth-grade students.* Pittsburgh, PA: University of Pittsburgh, Learning Research and Development Center.

Beck, I. L., & McKeown, M. G. (1991). Conditions of vocabulary acquisition. In P. D. Pearson (Eds.), *Handbook of reading research, Vol. 2* (pp. 789–814). New York: Longman.

Beck, I. L., & McKeown, M. G. (2001). Text talk: Capturing the benefits of read-aloud experiences for young children. *The Reading Teacher, 55,* 10–20.

Beck, I. L., & McKeown, M. G. (2004). *Increasing young children's oral vocabulary repertoires through rich and focused instruction.* Unpublished manuscript, University of Pittsburgh, Learning Research and Development Center.

Beck, I. L., McKeown, M. G., & Kucan, L. (2002). *Bringing words to life: Robust vocabulary instruction.* New York: Guilford Press.

Beck, I. L., McKeown, M .G., McCaslin, E. S., & Burkes, A. M. (1979). *Instructional dimensions that may affect reading comprehension: Examples from two commercial reading programs* (LRDC Publication No. 1979-20). Pittsburgh, PA: University of Pittsburgh, PA: Learning Research and Development Center.

Beck, I. L., McKeown, M. G., & Omanson, R. C. (1987). The effects and uses of diverse vocabulary instructional techniques. In M. G. McKeown & M. E. Curtis (Eds.), *The nature of vocabulary acquisition* (pp. 147–163). Hillsdale, NJ: Erlbaum.

Beck, I. L., Perfetti, C. A., & McKeown, M. G. (1982). The effects of long-term vocabulary instruction on lexical access and reading comprehension. *Journal of Educational Psychology, 74,* 506–521.

Becker, W. C. (1977). Teaching reading and language to the disadvantaged—What we have learned from field research. *Harvard Educational Review, 47,* 511–543.

Berko, J. (1958). The child's learning of English morphology. *Word, 14,* 150–177.

Biemiller, A. (1999). *Language and reading success.* Cambridge, MA: Brookline Books.

Biemiller, A. (2001, Spring). Teaching vocabulary: Early, direct, and sequential. *American Educator, 25* (1), 24–28, 47.

Biemiller, A. (2003, April). *Teaching vocabulary to kindergarten to grade two children.* Paper presented at the annual meeting of the American Educational Research Association, Chicago.

Biemiller, A. (2004). Teaching vocabulary in the primary grades: Vocabulary instruction needed. In J. F. Baumann & E. J. Kame'enui (Eds.), *Vocabulary instruction: Research to practice* (pp. 28–40). New York: Guilford Press.

Biemiller, A. (2005). Addressing developmental patterns in vocabulary: Implications for choosing words for primary grade vocabulary instruction. In E. H. Hiebert & M. L. Kamil (Eds.), *Teaching and learning vocabulary: Bringing research to practice* (pp. 209–242). Mahwah, NJ: Erlbaum.

Biemiller, A., & Boote, C. (2004). *An effective method for building vocabulary in primary grades.* Unpublished manuscript, University of Toronto, Canada.

Biemiller, A., & Slonim, N. (2001). Estimating root word and normative vocabulary growth in normative and advanced populations: Evidence for a common sequence of vocabulary acquisition. *Journal of Educational Psychology, 93,* 498–520.

Blachowicz, C., & Fisher, P. (1996). *Teaching vocabulary in all classrooms.* Columbus, OH: Merrill.

Blachowicz, C., & Fisher, P. (2000). Vocabulary instruction. In M. L. Kamil, P. Mosenthal, P. D. Pearson, & R. Barr (Eds.), *Handbook of reading research, Vol. 3* (pp. 503–523). Mahwah, NJ: Erlbaum.

Blachowicz, C., & Fisher, P. (2004). Keep the "fun" in fundamental: Encouraging words awareness and incidental word learning in the classroom through word play. In J. F. Baumann & E. J. Kame'enui (Eds.), *Vocabulary instruction: Research to practice* (pp. 218–237). New York: Guilford Press.

Blachowicz, C., & Zabroske, B. (1990). Context instruction: A metacognitive approach for at-risk readers. *Journal of Reading, 33,* 504–508.

Bos, C. S., Allen, A. A., & Scanlon, D. (1989). Vocabulary instruction and reading comprehension with bilingual learning disabled students. In S. McCormick & J. Zutell (Eds.), *Cognitive and social perspectives for literacy research and instruction* (pp. 173–178). Chicago: National Reading Conference.

Brown, A. L., & Campione, J. C. (1990). Interactive learning environments and the teaching of science and mathematics. In M. Gardner, J. G. Greeno, F. Reif, A. H. Schoenfeld, A. diSessa, & E. Sage (Eds.), *Toward a scientific practice of science education* (pp. 111–139). Hillsdale, NJ: Erlbaum.

Brown, R., Pressley, M., Van Meter, P., & Schuder, T. (1996). A quasi-experimental validation of transactional strategies instruction with low-achieving second grade readers. *Journal of Educational Psychology, 88,* 18–37.

Buikema, J. A., & Graves, M. F. (1993). Teaching students to use context cues to infer word meanings. *Journal of Reading, 36,* 450–457.

Calfee, R. C., & Drum, P. A. (1986). Research on teaching reading. In M. D. Wittrock (Ed.), *Handbook of research on teaching* (3rd ed., pp. 804–849). New York: Macmillan.

Carlo, M. S., August, D., McGlaughlin, B., Snow, C. E., Dressler, C., Lippman, D. N., Lively, T. J., & White, C. E. (2004). Closing the gap: Addressing the vocabulary needs of English-language learners in bilingual and mainstream classes. *Reading Research Quarterly, 39,* 188–215.

Carlo, M. S., August, D., & Snow, C. E. (2005). Sustained vocabulary-learning strategies for English language learners. In E. H. Hiebert & M. Kamil (Eds.), *Teaching and learning vocabulary: Bringing research to practice* (pp. 137–153). Mahwah, NJ: Erlbaum.

Carnine, D., Kame'enui, E. J., & Coyle, G. (1984). Utilization of contextual information in determining the meaning of unfamiliar words in context. *Reading Research Quarterly, 19*, 188–202.

Carroll, J. B., Davies, P., & Richman, B. (1971). *The American Heritage word frequency book.* New York: Houghton Mifflin.

Caroll, B. A., & Drum, P. A. (1983). Definitional gains from explicit and implicit context clues. In J. A. Niles & L. A. Harris (Eds.), *Yearbook of the National Reading Conference: Vol. 32. Searches for meaning in reading/ language processing & instruction* (pp. 158–162). Rochester, NY: National Reading Conference.

Chall, J. S., & Dale, E. (1995). *Readability revisited: The new Dale-Chall readability formula.* Cambridge, MA: Brookline Books.

Chall, J. S., Jacobs, V. A., & Baldwin, L. E. (1990). *The reading crisis: Why poor children fall behind.* Cambridge, MA: Harvard University Press.

Clark, E. V. (1993). *The lexicon in acquisition.* Cambridge, England: Cambridge University Press.

Clifford, G. J. (1978). Words for schools: The applications in education of the vocabulary researches of Edward L. Thorndike. In P. Suppes (Ed.), *Impact of research on education: Some case studies* (pp. 107–198). Washington, DC: National Academy of Education.

Collins COBUILD new student's dictionary (2002). (2nd ed.). Glasglow, Scotland: HarperCollins.

Coxhead, A. (2000). A new academic word list. *TESOL Quarterly 34*, 213–238.

Coyne, M. D., Simmons, D. C., & Kame'enui, E. J. (2004). Vocabulary instruction for young children at risk of experiencing reading difficulties: Teaching word meanings during shared storybook reading. In J. F. Baumann & E. J. Kame'enui (Eds.), *Vocabulary instruction: Research to practice* (pp. 41–58). New York: Guilford Press.

Cronbach, L. J. (1942). An analysis of techniques for diagnostic vocabulary testing. *Journal of Educational Research, 36*, 206–217.

Cummins, J. (2003). Reading and the bilingual student: Fact and friction. In G. G. Garcia (Ed.), *English learners: Reaching the highest level of English literacy* (pp. 2–33). Newark, DE: International Reading Association.

Cunningham, A. E., & Stanovich, K. E. (1997). Early reading acquisition and its relationship to reading experience and ability 10 years later. *Developmental Psychology, 33*, 934–945.

Cunningham, A. E., & Stanovich, K. E. (1998, Spring/Summer). What reading does for the mind. *American Educator, 22* (1/2), 8–15.

Dale, E. (1965). Vocabulary measurement: Techniques and major findings, *Elementary English, 42*, 82–88.

Dale, E., & O'Rourke, J. (1981). *The living word vocabulary.* Chicago: World Book-Childcraft International.

Dale, E., O'Rourke, J., & Bamman, H. A. (1971). *Techniques of teaching vocabulary*. Menlo Park, CA: Benjamin/Cummings.

De Temple, J., & Snow, C. E. (2003). Learning words from books. In A. van Kleeck, S. A. Stahl, & E. B. Bauer (Eds.), *On reading books to children: Parents and teachers* (pp. 16–36). Mahwah, NJ: Erlbaum.

Duffy, G. G. (2002). The case for direct explanation of strategies. In C. C. Block & M. Pressley (Eds.), *Comprehension instruction: Research-based best practices* (pp. 28–41). New York: Guilford Press.

Duffy, G. G., Roehler, L. R., Sivan, E., Rackliffe, G., Book, C., Meloth, M., Vavrus, L. G., Wesselman, R., Putnam, J., & Bassiri, D. (1987). Effects of explaining the reasoning associated with using reading strategies. *Reading Research Quarterly, 22*, 347–368.

Duin, A. H., & Graves, M. F. (1987). The effects of intensive vocabulary instruction on expository writing. *Reading Research Quarterly, 22*, 311–330.

Duin, A. H., & Graves, M. F. (1988). Teaching vocabulary as a writing prompt. *Journal of Reading, 22*, 204–212.

Duke, N. K., & Pearson, P. D. (2002). Effective practices for developing reading comprehension. In A. E. Farstrup & S. J. Samuels (Eds.), *What research has to say about reading instruction* (3rd ed., pp. 204–242). Newark, DE: International Reading Association.

Dupuy, H. (1974). *The rationale, development, and standardization of a basic word vocabulary test* (DHEW Publication No. HRA74-1334). Washington, DC: U.S. Government Printing Office.

Durkin, D. (1978/79). What classroom observations reveal about comprehension instruction. *Reading Research Quarterly, 14*, 481–533.

Durkin, D. (1981). Reading comprehension instruction in five basal reader series. *Reading Research Quarterly, 16*, 515–544.

Edwards, E. C., Font, G., Baumann, J. F., & Boland, E. (2004). Unlocking word meanings: Strategies and guidelines for teaching morphemic and contextual analysis. In J. F. Baumann & E. B. Kame'enui (Eds.), *Vocabulary instruction: Research to practice* (pp. 159–176). New York: Guilford Press.

Elley, W. B. (1996). Using book floods to raise literacy levels in developing countries. In V. Greaney (Ed.), *Promoting reading in developing countries* (pp. 148–162). Newark, DE: International Reading Association.

Fitzgerald, J. (1995). English as a second language instruction in the United States: A research review. *Journal of Reading Behavior, 27*, 115–152.

Flesch, R., & Lass, A. H. (1996). *The classic guide to better writing*. New York: HarperPerennial.

Folse, K. S. (2004). *Vocabulary myths: Applying second language research to classroom teaching*. Ann Arbor: University of Michigan Press.

Frayer, D. A., Frederick, W. D., & Klausmeier, H. J. (1969). *A schema for testing the level of concept mastery* (Working Paper No. 16). Madison: Wisconsin Research and Development Center for Cognitive Learning.

Freyd, P., & Baron, J. (1982). Individual differences in acquisition of derivational morphology. *Journal of Verbal Learning and Verbal Behavior, 21*, 282–295.

Fry, E. B. (2004). *The vocabulary teacher's book of lists*. San Francisco: Jossey-Bass.

Fukkink, R. G., & de Glopper, K. (1998). Effects of instruction in deriving word meanings from context: A meta-analysis. *Review of Educational Research, 68*, 450–469.

Garcia, G. E. (1991). Factors influencing the English reading test performance of Spanish-speaking Hispanic students. *Reading Research Quarterly, 26*, 371–392.

Garcia, G. E. (1996, December). *Improving the English reading of Mexican-American bilingual students through the use of cognate recognition strategies.* Paper presented at the National Reading Conference, Charleston, SC.

Gersten, R., & Baker, S. (2000). What we know about effective instructional practices for English-language learners. *Exceptional Children, 66*, 454–470.

Goswami, U. (2001). Early phonological development and the acquisition of literacy. In S. B. Neuman & D. K. Dickinson (Eds.), *Handbook of early literacy research* (pp. 111–125). New York: Guilford Press.

Graves, M. F. (1984). Selecting vocabulary to teach in the intermediate and secondary grades. In J. Flood (Ed.), *Understanding reading comprehension* (pp. 245–260). Newark, DE: International Reading Association.

Graves, M. F. (1985). *A word is a word . . . or is it.* New York: Scholastic.

Graves, M. F. (1986). Vocabulary learning and instruction. In E. Z. Rothkopf (Ed.), *Review of Research in Education* (Vol. 13, pp. 49–90). Washington, DC: American Educational Research Association.

Graves, M. F. (1987). The role of instruction in vocabulary development. In M. G. McKeown & M. E. Curtis (Eds.), *The nature of vocabulary acquisition* (pp. 165–184). Hillsdale, NJ: Erlbaum.

Graves, M. F. (1992). The elementary vocabulary curriculum: What should it be? In M. J. Dreher & W. H. Slater (Eds.), *Elementary school literacy: Critical issues* (pp. 101–131). Norwood, MA: Christopher-Gordon.

Graves, M. F. (2000). A vocabulary program to complement and bolster a middle-grade comprehension program. In B. M. Taylor, M. F. Graves, & P. van den Broek (Eds.), *Reading for meaning: Fostering comprehension in the middle grades* (pp. 116–135). New York: Teachers College Press.

Graves, M. F. (2004). Teaching prefixes: As good as it gets?. In J. F. Baumann & E. B. Kame'enui (Eds.), *Vocabulary instruction: Research to practice* (pp. 81–99). New York: Guilford Press.

Graves, M. F., & Fitzgerald, J. (in press). What are the components of a comprehensive program to help English-language learners achieve vocabulary success? In C. C. Block & J. Mangieri (Eds.), *Strategies for Vocabulary Success.* New York: Scholastic.

Graves, M. F., & Gebhart, D. V. (1982). Content teachers' predictions of students' knowledge of specific words. *Reading Psychology, 3*, 211–220.

Graves, M. F., & Hammond, H. K. (1980). A validated procedure for teaching prefixes and its effect on students' ability to assign meaning to novel words.

In M. L. Kamil & A. J. Moe (Eds.), *Perspectives on reading research and instruction* (pp. 184–188). Washington, DC: National Reading Conference.

Graves, M. F., Juel, C., & Graves, B. B. (Eds.). (2004). *Teaching reading in the 21st century* (3rd ed.). Boston: Allyn & Bacon.

Graves, M. F., & Slater, W. H. (in press). Vocabulary instruction in content areas. In D. Lapp, J. Flood, & N. Farnan (Eds.), *Content area reading and learning: Instructional strategies* (3rd ed.). Mahwah, NJ: Erlbaum.

Graves, M. F., & Watts, S. M. (2002). The place of word consciousness in a research-based vocabulary program. In S. J. Samuels & A. E. Farstrup (Eds.), *What research has to say about reading instruction* (3rd ed., pp. 140–165). Newark, DE: International Reading Association.

Greenman, R. (2000). *Words that make a difference and how to use them in a masterly way.* Delray Beach, FL: Levenger Press.

Hart, B., & Risley, T. R. (1995). *Meaningful differences in the everyday experiences of young American children.* Baltimore: P. H. Brookes.

Hart, B., & Risley, T. R. (2003, Spring). The early catastrophe: The 30 million word gap. *American Educator, 27*(1), 4–9.

Hartman, G. W. (1946). Further evidence of the unexpected large size of recognition vocabularies among college students. *Journal of Educational Psychology, 37,* 436–439.

Hayes, D. P., & Ahrens, M. (1988). Vocabulary simplification for children: A special case of "motherese"? *Journal of Child Language, 15,* 395–410.

Heimlich, J. E., & Pittelman, S. D. (1986). *Semantic mapping: Classroom applications.* Newark, DE: International Reading Association.

Herman, P. A., & Dole, J. (1988). Theory and practice in vocabulary learning and instruction. *Elementary School Journal, 89,* 43–54.

Hiebert, E. H. (2005). In pursuit of an effective, efficient vocabulary program. To appear in E. H. Hiebert & M. L. Kamil (Eds.), *Teaching and learning vocabulary: Bringing research to practice* (pp. 243–263). Mahwah, NJ: Erlbaum.

Hirsch, E. D. (2003, Spring). Reading comprehension requires knowledge—of words and the world. *American Educator, 27*(1), 10–13, 16–22, 28–29, 44.

Jenkins, J. R., & Dixon, R. (1983). Vocabulary learning. *Contemporary Educational Psychology, 8,* 237–260.

Jenkins, J. R., Stein, M. L., & Wysocki, K. (1984). Learning vocabulary through reading. *American Educational Research Journal, 21,* 767–787.

Jenkins, J. R., & Wysocki, K. (1985). *Deriving word meanings from context.* Unpublished manuscript, University of Washington, Seattle.

Jimémez, R. T., Garcia, G. E., & Pearson, P. D. (1996). The reading strategies of Latina/o students who are successful English readers: Opportunities and obstacles. *Reading Research Quarterly, 31,* 90–112.

Johnson, D. D., Johnson, B. V. H., & Schlichting, K. (2004). Logology: Word and language play. In J. F. Baumann & E. J. Kame'enui (Eds.), *Vocabulary instruction: Research to practice* (pp. 179–200). New York: Guilford Press.

Johnson, D. D., Toms-Bronowski, S., & Pittelman, S. D. (1982). *An investigation of the effectiveness of semantic mapping and semantic feature analy-*

sis with intermediate grade level children. (Program Report No. 83-3).
Madison: Wisconsin Center for Education Research.

Juel, C., & Deffes, R. (2004). Making words stick. *Educational Leadership, 61*
(6), 30–34.

Kame'enui, E. J., & Baumann, J. F. (2004). Vocabulary: The plot of the reading
story. In J. F. Baumann & E. J. Kame'enui (Eds.), *Vocabulary instruction:
Research to practice* (pp. 3–10). New York: Guilford Press.

Kamil, M. L., & Bernhardt, E. B. (2004). Reading instruction for English-language learners. In M. F. Graves, C. Juel, & B. B. Graves (Eds.), *Teaching
reading in the 21st century* (3rd ed.). Boston: Allyn & Bacon.

Kamil, M. L., & Hiebert, E. H. (2005). The teaching and learning of vocabulary: Perspectives and persistent issues. In E. H. Hiebert & M. L. Kamil
(Eds.), *Teaching and learning vocabulary: Bringing research to practice*
(pp. 1–23). Mahwah, NJ: Erlbaum.

Katch, J. (2004). The most important words. *Educational Leadership, 61*(6), 62–
64.

Kaye, D. B., & Sternberg, R. J. (1982). *The development of lexical decomposi-
tion ability.* Unpublished manuscript.

Klare, G. R. (1984). Readability. In P. D. Pearson, R. Barr, M. L. Kamil, & P.
Mosenthal (Eds.), *Handbook of reading research* (pp. 681–794). New York:
Longman.

Kuhn, M. R., & Stahl, S. A. (1998). Teaching children to learn word meanings
from context: A synthesis and some questions. *Journal of Literacy Research, 30,* 119–138.

LaBerge, D., & Samuels, S. J. (1974). Toward a theory of automatic information processing in reading. *Cognitive Psychology, 6,* 293–323.

Lederer, R. (1988). *Get thee to a punnery.* Charleston, SC: Wyrick.

Lederer, R. (1996). *Pun and games.* Chicago: Chicago Review Press.

Long, M. H., & Richards, J. C. (2001). Series editor's preface. In I. S. P. Nation,
Learning vocabulary in another language (p. xiii). Cambridge, UK: Cambridge University Press.

Longman American idioms dictionary. (1999). Harlow, England: Pearson
Education.

Lorge, I., & Chall, J. (1963). Estimating the size of vocabularies of children and
adults: An analysis of methodological issues. *Journal of Experimental
Education, 32,* 147–157.

McKeown, M. G. (1993). Creating effective definitions for young word learners. *Reading Research Quarterly, 28,* 16–31.

McKeown, M. G., & Beck, I. L. (2003). Taking advantage of read alongs to help
children make sense of decontextualized language. In A. van Kleeck, S. A.
Stahl, & E. B. Bauer (Eds.), *On reading books to children: Parents and
teachers* (pp. 159–176). Mahwah, NJ: Erlbaum.

McKeown, M. G., & Beck, I. L. (2004). Direct and rich vocabulary instruction.
In J. F. Baumann & E. B. Kame'enui (Eds.), *Vocabulary instruction: Research to practice* (pp. 13–27). New York: Guilford Press.

McKeown, M. G., Beck, I. L., Omanson, R. C., & Perfetti, C. A. (1983). The effects of long-term vocabulary instruction on reading comprehension: A replication. *Journal of Reading Behavior, 15,* 3–18.

McKeown, M. G., Beck, I. L., Omanson, R. C., & Pople, M. T. (1985). Some effects of the nature and frequency of vocabulary instruction on the knowledge and use of words. *Reading Research Quarterly, 20,* 522–535.

Mezynski, K. (1983). Issues concerning the acquisition of knowledge: Effects of vocabulary training on reading comprehension. *Review of Educational Research, 53,* 253–279.

Microsoft Corp. (2001). Microsoft Word X for Mac. [Computer software]. Redmond, WA: Author.

Miller, G. A., & Gildea, P. M. (1987). How children learn words. *Scientific American, 257*(3), 94–99.

Miller, G. A., & Wakefield, P. C. (1993). Commentary on Anglin's analysis of vocabulary growth. In J. M. Anglin, Vocabulary development: A Morphological analysis. *Monographs of the Society for Research in Child Development, 58*(10, Serial No. 238), 167–175.

Moll, L. C. (1988). Some key issues in teaching Latino students. *Language Arts, 65,* 465–472.

Nagy, W. E. (1988). *Teaching vocabulary to improve reading comprehension.* Newark, DE: International Reading Association.

Nagy, W. E. (2005). Why vocabulary instruction needs to be long-term and comprehensive. In E. Hiebert & M. L. Kamil (Eds.), *Teaching and learning vocabulary: Bringing research to practice* (pp. 27–44). Mahwah, NJ: Erlbaum.

Nagy, W. E. (in press). Metalinguistic awareness and the vocabulary-comprehension connection. In R. Wagner (Ed.), *Vocabulary and reading.* New York: Guilford Press.

Nagy, W. E., & Anderson, R. C. (1984). How many words are there in printed school English? *Reading Research Quarterly, 19,* 304–330.

Nagy, W. E., Anderson, R. C., & Herman, P. A. (1987). Learning word meanings from context during normal reading. *American Educational Research Journal, 24,* 237–270.

Nagy, W. E., Anderson, R. C., Schommer, M., Scott, J. A., & Stallman, A. C. (1989). Morphological families in the internal lexicon. *Reading Research Quarterly, 24,* 262–282.

Nagy, W. E., Diakidoy, I. N., & Anderson, R. C. (1993). The acquisition of morphology: Learning the contributions of suffixes to the meanings of derivatives. *Journal of Reading Behavior, 25,* 155–170.

Nagy, W. E., Garcia, G. E., Durgunoglu, A., & Hancin-Bhatt, B. (1993). Spanish-English bilingual children's use and recognition of cognates in English reading. *Journal of Reading Behavior, 25,* 241–259.

Nagy, W. E., & Herman, P. A. (1987). Breadth and depth of vocabulary knowledge: Implications for acquisition and instruction. In M. G. McKeown & M. E. Curtis (Eds.), *The nature of vocabulary acquisition* (pp. 19–35). Hillsdale, NJ: Erlbaum.

Nagy, W. E., Herman, P. A., & Anderson, R. C. (1985). Learning words from context. *Reading Research Quarterly, 20,* 233–253.

Nagy, W. E., & Scott, J. A. (2000). Vocabulary processes. In R. Barr, M. L. Kamil, P. Mosenthal, & P. D. Pearson (Eds.), *Handbook of reading research Vol. 3* (pp. 269–284). New York: Longman.

Nation, I. S. P. (2001). *Learning vocabulary in another language.* Cambridge, U.K.: Cambridge University Press.

National Assessment of Educational Progress. (2003). *The nation's report card.* Retrieved July 1, 2004, from http://nces.ed.gov/nationsreportcard/naepdata

National Reading Panel. (2000). *Report of the National Reading Panel: Teaching children to read.* Bethesda, MD: National Institute of Child Health and Human Development.

National Research Council. (2004). *Engaging schools: Fostering high school students' motivation to learn.* Washington, DC: National Academies Press.

Neuman, S. B., & Celano, D. (2001). Access to print in low-income and middle-income communities: An ecological study of four neighborhoods. *Reading Research Quarterly, 36,* 8–26.

Nicol, J. A., Graves, M. F., & Slater, W. H. (1984). *Building vocabulary through prefix instruction.* Unpublished manuscript, University of Minnesota, Minneapolis.

Nicol, J. A. (1980). *Effects of prefix instruction on students' vocabulary size.* Unpublished master's thesis, University of Minnesota, Minneapolis.

Nist, S. L., & Olejnik, S. (1995). The role of context and dictionary definitions on various levels of word knowledge. *Reading Research Quarterly, 30,* 172–193.

O'Rourke, J. P. (1974). *Toward a science of vocabulary development.* The Hague: Mouton.

Osborn, J., & Lehr, F. (in press). *A focus on vocabulary.* Honolulu, HI: Pacific Resources for Education and Learning.

Paris, S. G., Lipson, M. Y., & Wixson, K. S. (1983). Becoming a strategic reader. *Contemporary Educational Psychology, 8,* 293–316.

Parker, S. L. (1984). *A comparison of four types of initial vocabulary instruction.* Unpublished master's thesis, University of Minnesota, Minneapolis.

Patberg, J. P., Graves, M. F., & Stibbe, M. A. (1984). Effects of active teaching and practice in facilitating students' use of context clues. In J. A. Niles & L. A. Harris (Eds.), *Yearbook of the National Reading Conference: Vol. 33. Changing perspectives in research in reading/language processing and instruction* (pp. 146–151). Rochester, NY: National Reading Conference.

Patberg, J. P., & Stibbe, M. A. (1985, December). *The effects of contextual analysis instruction on vocabulary learning.* Paper presented at the annual meeting of the National Reading Conference, San Diego, CA.

Pearson, P. D., Roehler, L .R., Dole, J. A., & Duffy, G. G. (1992). Developing expertise in reading comprehension. In S. J. Samuels & A. E. Farstrup (Eds.), *What research has to say about reading instruction* (2nd ed., pp. 145–199). Newark, DE: International Reading Association.

Perez, E. (1981). Oral language competence improves reading skills of Mexican-American third graders. *The Reading Teacher, 35,* 24–27.

Petty, W., Herold, C., & Stoll, E. (1967). *The state of knowledge about the teaching of vocabulary.* Urbana, IL: National Council of Teachers of English.

Pinker, S. (2000). *The language instinct: How the mind creates language.* New York: Perennial Classics.

Pittelman, S. D., Heimlich, J. E., Berglund, R. L., & French, M. P. (1991). *Semantic feature analysis: Classroom applications.* Newark, DE: International Reading Association.

Pressley, M. (2000). What should reading comprehension instruction be the instruction of? In M. L. Kamil, P. Mosenthal, P. D. Pearson, & R. Barr (Eds.), *Handbook of reading research, Vol. 3* (pp. 545–561). Mahwah, NJ: Erlbaum.

Pressley, M. (2002). Comprehension strategies instruction: A turn of the century report. In C. C. Block & M. Pressley (Eds.), *Comprehension instruction: Research-based best practices* (pp. 11–27). New York: Guilford Press.

Pressley, M., Dolezal, S. E., Raphael, L. M., Mohan, L., Roehrig, A. D., & Bogner, K. (2003). *Motivating primary-grade students.* New York: Guilford Press.

Pressley, M., & El-Dinary, P. B. (1997). What we know about translating comprehension strategies instruction research into practice. *Journal of Learning Disabilities, 30,* 486–488.

Pressley, M., El-Dinary, P. B., Gaskins, I., Schuder, T., Bergman, J. L., Almasi, J., & Brown, R. (1992). Beyond direct explanation: Transactional instruction of reading comprehension strategies. *Elementary School Journal, 92,* 511–554.

Pressley, M., Harris, K. R., & Marks, M. B. (1992). But good strategy instructors are constructivists! *Educational Psychology Review, 4,* 3–31.

RAND Reading Study Group. (2002). *Reading for understanding: Toward an R&D program in reading comprehension.* Santa Monica, CA: RAND Education.

Rasmussen, S., & Oosterman, D. (1999). *Lexical procurement (vocabulary).* Unpublished manuscript.

Read together, talk together: Parent video. (2002). New York: Pearson Early Learning.

Read together, talk together: Teacher training video. (2002). New York: Pearson Early Learning.

Reese, E., & Cox, A. (1999). Quality of adult book reading affects children's emergent literacy. *Developmental Psychology, 35,* 20–28.

Reutzel, D. R., Fawson, P. C., & Smith, J. A. (2003, December). *Teaching comprehension strategies using information texts.* Paper presented at the annual meeting of the National Reading Conference, Scottsdale, AZ.

Roser, N., & Juel, C. (1982). Effects of vocabulary instruction on reading comprehension. In J. A. Niles & L. A. Harris (Eds.), *Yearbook of the National Reading Conference: Vol. 31. New inquiries in reading research and instruction* (pp. 110–118). Rochester, NY: National Reading Conference.

Ryder, R. J., & Graves, M. F. (1994). Vocabulary instruction presented prior to reading in two basal readers. *Elementary School Journal, 95,* 139–153.

Ryder, R. J., & Graves, M. F. (2003). *Reading and learning in content areas* (3rd ed.). Columbus, OH: Merrill; New York: Wiley.

Sales, G. C., & Graves, M. F. (2005). *Teaching reading comprehension strategies*. (U.S. Department of Education Project Number R3055040194). Minneapolis, MN: Seward Incorporated.

Scarborough, H. S. (1998). Early identification of children at risk for reading disabilities: Phonological awareness and some other promising predictors. In B. K. Shapiro, P. J. Accardo, & A. J. Capute (Eds.), *Specific reading disabilities: A review of the spectrum* (pp. 75–119). Timonium, MD: York Press.

Schmitt, N. (2000). *Vocabulary in language teaching*. Cambridge, UK: Cambridge University Press.

Scott, J. A., Blackstone, T., Cross, S., Jones, A., Skobel, B., Wells, J., & Jensen, Y. (1996, May). *The power of language: Creating contexts which enrich children's understanding and use of words*. Microworkshop conducted at the annual meeting of the International Reading Association, New Orleans, LA.

Scott, J. A., Butler, C., & Asselin, M. (1996, December). *The effect of mediated assistance in word learning*. Paper presented at the annual meeting of the National Reading Conference, Charleston, SC.

Scott, J. A., Jamieson-Noel, D., & Asselin, M. (2003). Vocabulary instruction throughout the day in twenty-three Canadian upper-elementary classrooms. *Elementary School Journal, 103,* 269–286.

Scott, J. A., Jones, A., Blackstone, T., Cross, S., Skobel, B., & Hayes, E. (1994, May). *A gift of words: Creating a context for rich language use*. Microworkshop conducted at the meeting of the International Reading Association, Toronto, Canada.

Scott, J. A., & Nagy, W. E. (1997). Understanding the definitions of unfamiliar verbs. *Reading Research Quarterly, 32,* 184–200.

Scott, J. A., & Nagy, W. E. (2004). Developing word consciousness. In J. F. Baumann & E. J. Kame'enui (Eds.), *Vocabulary instruction: Research to practice* (pp. 201–217). New York: Guilford Press.

Scott, J. A., & Wells, J. (1998). Readers take responsibility: Literature circles and the growth of critical thinking. In K. Beers & B. Samuels (Eds.), *Into focus: Understanding and supporting middle school readers*. Norwood, MA: Christopher-Gordon.

Shefelbine, J. L. (1983, April). *Learning word meanings from context*. Paper presented at the annual meeting of the American Educational Research Association, Montreal, Canada.

Shibles, B. H. (1959). How many words does the first grade child know? *Elementary English, 31,* 42–47.

Slavin, R. E., & Cheung, A. (2003). *Effective reading programs for English language learners: A best-evidence synthesis*. Baltimore, MD: Johns Hopkins University, Center for the Education of Students Placed at Risk.

Stahl, S. A. (1983). Differential word knowledge and reading comprehension. *Journal of Reading Behavior, 15,* 33–50.

Stahl, S. A. (1998). Four questions about vocabulary. In C. R. Hynd (Ed.), *Learning from text across conceptual domains* (pp. 73–94). Mahway, NJ: Erlbaum.

Stahl, S. A., & Fairbanks, M. M. (1986). The effects of vocabulary instruction: A model-based meta-analysis. *Review of Educational Research, 56*, 72–110.

Stahl, S. A., & Kapinus, B. (1991). Possible sentences: Predicting word meanings to teach content area vocabulary. *The Reading Teacher, 45*, 36–43.

Stahl, S. A., & Stahl, K. D. (2004). Word wizards all!: Teaching word meanings in preschool and primary education. In In J. F. Baumann & E. B. Kame'enui (Eds), *Vocabulary instruction: Research to practice* (pp. 59–78). New York: Guilford Press.

Sternberg, R. J. (1987). Most vocabulary is learned from context. In M. G. McKeown & M. E. Curtis (Eds.), *The nature of vocabulary acquisition* (pp. 89–105). Hillsdale, NJ: Erlbaum.

Swanborn, M. S. W., & de Glopper, K. (1999). Incidental word learning while reading: A meta-analysis. *Review of Educational Research, 69*, 261–285.

Sweet, A. P., & Snow, C. E. (2003). *Rethinking reading comprehension.* New York: Guilford Press.

Templin, M. C. (1957). *Certain language skills in children, their development and interrelationships.* Minneapolis: University of Minnesota Press.

Terman, L. M. (1916). *The measurement of intelligence.* Boston: Houghton Mifflin.

Thorndike, E. L. (1941). *The teaching of English suffixes.* New York: Teachers College, Columbia University.

Vygotsky, L. S. (1978). *Mind in society: The development of higher psychological processes.* Cambridge, MA: Harvard University Press.

Walsh, K. (2003, Spring). Basal readers: The lost opportunity to build the knowledge that propels comprehension. *American Educator, 27*(1), 24–27.

Watts, S. M. (1995). Vocabulary instruction during reading lessons in six classrooms. *Journal of Reading Behavior, 27*, 399–424.

Weizman, Z. O., & Snow, C. E. (2001). Lexical imput as related to children's vocabulary acquisition: Effects of sophisticated exposure and support for meaning. *Developmental Psychology, 37*, 265–279.

Werner, H., & Kaplan, E. (1952). The acquisition of word meanings: A developmental study. *Monographs of the Society for Research in Child Development, 15*(1), Serial No. 238.

West, M. (1953). *A general service list of English words.* London: Longmans, Green, and Company.

White, T. G., Graves, M. F., & Slater, W. H. (1990). Growth of reading vocabulary in diverse elementary schools: Decoding and word meaning. *Journal of Educational Psychology, 82*, 281–290.

White, T. G., Power, M. A., & White, S. (1989). Morphological analysis: Implication for teaching and understanding vocabulary growth. *Reading Research Quarterly, 24*, 283–304

White, T. G., Slater, W. H., & Graves, M .F. (1989). Yes/no method of vocabulary assessment: Valid for whom and useful for what? In S. McCormick & J. Zutell (Eds.), *Yearbook of the National Reading Conference: Vol. 38. Cognitive and social perspectives for literacy research and instruction* (pp. 391–398). Chicago: National Reading Conference.

White, T. G., Sowell, J., & Yanagihara, A. (1989). Teaching elementary students to use word-part clues. *The Reading Teacher, 42,* 302–308.

Whitehurst, G. J., Arnold, D. S., Epstein, J. N., Angell, A. L., Smith, M., & Fischel, J. E. (1994). A picture book reading intervention in day care and home for children from low-income families. *Developmental Psychology, 30,* 697–689.

Whitehurst, G. J., Falcon, F., Lonigan, C. J., Fischel, J. E., DeBaryshe, D. B., Valdez-Menchaca, M. C., & Caulfield, M. (1988). Accelerating language development through picture book reading. *Developmental Psychology, 24,* 552–559.

Wigfield, A., & Eccles, J. S. (Eds.). (2002). *Development of achievement motivation.* San Diego: Academic Press.

Wiggins, G., & McTighe, J. (1998). *Understanding by design.* Alexandria, VA: Association for Supervision and Curriculum Development.

Wiske, M. S. (1998). *Teaching for understanding: Linking research with practice.* San Francisco: Jossey-Bass.

Wysocki, K., & Jenkins, J. R. (1987). Deriving word meanings through morphological generalization. *Reading Research Quarterly, 22,* 66–81.

Zeno, S. M., Ivens, S. H., Millard, R. T., & Duvvuri, R. (1995). *The educator's word frequency guide.* Brewster, NY: Touchstone Applied Science Associates.

Zevenbergen, A. A., & Whitehurst, G. J. (2003). Dialogic reading: A shared picture book reading intervention for preschoolers. In A. van Kleeck, S. A. Stahl, & E. B. Bauer (Eds.), *On reading books to children: Parents and teachers* (pp. 177–200). Mahwah, NJ: Erlbaum.

Index

NAMES

Ahrens, M., 41
Allen, A. A., 35
Alvermann, D. E., 5
Anders, P. L., 21
Anderson, Richard C., 3–5, 7, 13, 14, 24–25, 28, 32, 40–41, 61, 91, 103, 119
Andrews, Darcy, 148–151, 158
Andrews, L., 132, 136
Angell, A. L., 47–49
Anglin, J. M., 3–4, 7, 14, 27, 61
Arnold, D. H., 49
Arnold, D. S., 47–49
Ash, G. E., 4, 6, 19–21, 23, 25
Asselin, M., 6, 17–18, 33
August, D., 3, 4, 33–36, 86
Avi, 145

Babbitt, Natalie, 128–129
Baker, S., 86
Baldwin, L. E., 4, 18, 120
Bamman, H. A., 28–29
Baron, J., 28
Base, Graeme, 126
Bassiri, D., 92
Baumann, J. F., 4, 6–7, 19–21, 23, 25–27, 29–30, 32, 74
Beck, Garrard, 159
Beck, I. L., 3–6, 12, 16, 19, 21–23, 27, 32, 33, 39, 43–44, 46, 47, 52–54, 61, 68, 69, 74, 85, 127, 129, 134, 141–142
Becker, W. C., 3, 4, 18, 120
Berglund, R. L., 21, 80–81

Berko, J., 27
Bernhardt, E. B., 87
Biemiller, A., 3–6, 14, 18, 19, 43–44, 47, 49–52, 65, 66, 69, 120
Bigelow, Nancy, 140
Birdwell, Norman, 50
Blachowicz, C., 6–7, 19, 32, 123, 127
Blackstone, T., 121–122, 127
Bogner, K., 32, 120
Boland, E., 6–7, 23, 26, 27, 29–30
Book, C., 92
Boote, C., 50
Bos, C. S., 21, 35
Brown, A. L., 117–118
Brown, R., 92
Buikema, J. A., 6–7, 26
Burkes, A. M., 16
Butler, C., 33

Calfee, R. C., 12, 134
Campione, J. C., 117–118
Carlo, M. S., 3, 4, 33–36, 86
Carnine, D., 25, 27
Caroll, B. A., 24
Carroll, J. B., 13, 15, 24, 65
Caulfield, M., 18–19, 47–49
Celano, D., 42
Chall, J. S., 3, 4, 14, 18, 50, 66, 120
Cheung, A., 33–35, 86
Clark, E. V., 1, 27, 134
Clements, Andrew, 126
Clifford, G. J., 10
Cox, A., 46

Coxhead, A., 87
Coyle, G., 25, 27
Coyne, M. D., 3, 4
Creech, Sharon, 121
Cronbach, L. J., 12
Cross, S., 121–122, 127
Cummins, J., 34, 86–87
Cunningham, A. E., 3–5

Dale, E., 3, 28–29, 50, 66, 134
Davies, P., 13, 15, 65
DeBaryshe, D. B., 18–19, 47–49
Deffes, R., 19, 47, 54–56, 69, 71–72
de Glopper, K., 6, 23, 25–27
De Temple, J., 44–46
Diakidoy, I. N., 28
Dixon, R., 16
Dole, J. A., 6, 69, 92
Dolezal, S. E., 32, 120
Dressler, C., 3, 33–36, 86
Drum, P. A., 12, 24, 134
Duffy, G. G., 92
Duin, A. H., 33, 85–86, 127, 129–130
Duke, N. K., 92
Dupuy, H., 13–14
Durgunoglu, A., 34–35
Durkin, D., 6, 16, 17
Duvvuri, R., 13, 15, 130

Eccles, J. S., 120
Edwards, E. C., 6–7, 23, 26, 27, 29–30, 74
Einstein, Albert, 10
El-Dinary, P. B., 92, 93
Elley, W. B., 40
Epstein, J. N., 47–49

SUBJECTS

About the Author

Michael F. Graves is Professor of Literacy Education at the University of Minnesota. His research and development interests are in comprehension instruction and vocabulary development. He first began developing the vocabulary program described in this book in the 1980s. His other recent books include *Scaffolding Reading Experiences: Designs for Student Success* (2003, with Bonnie Graves), *Teaching Reading in the 21st Century* (with Connie Jael and Bonnie Graves), and *Reading and Responding in the Middle Grades* (in press, with Lee Galda).